Praise for *Screens and Teens*

As a dad trying to make sense of parenting in this brave new world, I read everything that Kathy Koch writes. Practical, thoughtful, hopeful, and enjoyable, she is a wise guide. And I found *Screens and Teens* to be her best book yet. Parenting today means understanding what technology and media do to us and to our kids, and knowing what to do in light of the challenges. This book offers both.

—**JOHN STONESTREET**, speaker and fellow, the Chuck Colson Center for Christian Worldview, and senior content advisor, Summit Ministries

Technology has changed our world big time. Although tempted, even if I could, I wouldn't turn back the hands of time. For instance, I'm glad I have a cellphone. I'm glad I have access to the Internet. For the most part, I'm glad for Facebook and Twitter. But not everything that goes with this digital revolution is a good thing. How many people in your church are checking emails during the Sunday sermon? Ever see a family at a restaurant, all gazing at their phones with not a single word being spoken? *Screens and Teens*, helps us navigate this brave new world by helping us see the bigger picture—especially how ultimately media impacts character and spiritual maturity.

—**BOB WALISZEWSKI**, director, Plugged In, and author of *Plugged-In Parenting: How to Raise Media-Savvy Kids with Love, Not War*

Talking on a phone for hours isn't anything new for a teenager, but having a phone on 24/7 is. What's a parent to do in the face of this relentless fascination with screens? Enter Dr. Kathy. She has the uncanny ability to be an advocate for teens and parents alike. She will help you better understand your tech-savvy teen and show you how to meet your child's deepest needs (no phone required).

—**ARLENE PELLICANE**, coauthor, *Growing Up Social: Raising Relational Kids in a Screen-Driven World*

D1007322

In a world of ever-changing technology and cultural values, parents need wise voices, well-researched advice, and practical help as guardrails for their growing children. Kathy Koch, Celebrate Kids, and Hearts at Home are motivated, care about the children of this world, and walk alongside parents in helping guide them.

—**PAM FARREL**, author of *10 Best Decisions a Parent Can Make* and *10 Questions Kids Ask about Sex*

As Dr. Kathy Koch says in this important book, our kids don't think much about technology. It's their way of life, and using it is as natural as breathing. That doesn't mean they don't need help navigating this area of life. They do—just like all others—in a way that is healthy vs unhealthy. I must admit as a parent of a fifteen- and a twelve-year-old, I have been intimidated by not knowing how to do that. Now with this book I finally have an excellent tool that will make all the difference for me and my family.

—**SHAUNTI FELDHAHN**, social researcher and bestselling author of *For Women Only* and *For Parents Only*

Screens and Teens offers sound, sensible, and balanced advice for moms and dads swimming in the cyber seas of online concern. Deftly researched and written in an easy-to-digest manner, it's a wonderful what-to-do-and-consider reading application for parents everywhere.

—**JULIE BARNHILL**, speaker and author

From smartphones to computers to tablets to TVs, it seems like everything we do in life involves a screen. In *Screens and Teens*, Dr. Kathy Koch leaves readers with a strategy for success. Very quickly, she draws us in to the power of screens and the effect they have on our lives. And she's quick to point out that it's not just kids. Parents get sucked into screen time just as easily. Koch's presentation is quite balanced. She never errs on the side of condemning technology but instead is careful to present technology as a magnifier—it simply makes some mistakes easier to make. If you have a teen who's struggling with phone issues or simply wants to be proactive, this is the book to read.

—**JOSH OLDS**, LifeIsStory.com

SCREENS AND TEENS

CONNECTING WITH OUR KIDS
IN A WIRELESS WORLD

KATHY KOCH, PH.D.

MOODY PUBLISHERS

CHICAGO

Published in association with the literary agent Sandra Bishop

Edited by Annette LaPlaca
Interior design: Ragont Design
Cover design: Tobias Design, Inc.
Cover image: Christopher Tobias / Tobias' Outerwear for Books
Author Photo: Wayne Stratton Photography

Library of Congress Cataloging-in-Publication Data

Koch, Kathy.
  Screens and teens : connecting with our kids in a wireless world / Kathy Koch.
    pages cm
  Includes bibliographical references.
  ISBN 978-0-8024-1269-0 (paperback)
  1. Internet and children. 2. Social media. 3. Interpersonal relations in adolescence. 4. Self-actualization (Psychology) in adolescence. 5.Social media--Religious aspects. I. Title.
  HQ799.2.I5K63 2015
  004.67'8083--dc23
                           2014042103

We hope you enjoy this book from Moody Publishers. Our goal is to provide high-quality, thought-provoking books and products that connect truth to your real needs and challenges. For more information on other books and products written and produced from a biblical perspective, go to www.moodypublishers.com or write to:

Moody Publishers
820 N. LaSalle Boulevard
Chicago, IL 60610

3 5 7 9 10 8 6 4 2

Printed in the United States of America

To my brother, Dave, his wife, Debbie,
and their three children, Betsy, Katie, and Andy,
who pursue life, purpose, and fun with and without
screens and have mastered the art of conversation.
Our connections run deep and wide,
and I'm extremely grateful.

CONTENTS

FOREWORD

Less than twenty-four hours after we dropped him off at college our son began asking to come home. This wasn't what he thought it would look like. It was too hard. There were topics being taught that he didn't want to learn. "I want to come home," he texted every single day during the first week of school.

We listened, encouraged, spoke wisdom, and ultimately said, "You need to stay at least one semester." This was so hard! There were times my husband and I wanted to cave in and when we questioned if we were doing the right thing.

After a week, Mark and I made a call to the dean of students. He thanked us for the phone call, reassured us they could help from their end, and encouraged us that our "no" was exactly what our son needed. Then he said these words: "I'm finding that this generation of kids does not know how to persevere." We talked about how today's teens are accustomed to quick wins in front of a video game screen. They fix problems with one click to cut and another click to paste. Thanks to the Internet, information can be found at young people's fingertips without much effort to research, dig, and come to conclusions on their own. When fixes aren't so quick and easy, their first impulse is to give up.

Our ever-changing technology has, without a doubt, made our lives easier in many ways. But technology has also made some aspects of parenting harder and is affecting the minds, bodies, and souls of our kids in ways we desperately need to understand.

Should we box up our computers and cellphones and return to encyclopedias and landlines? That's not the answer. Technology will only move forward, and we have to move forward with it. We do, however, have to change the way we interact with our kids. We have to give them opportunities to persevere. We have to teach them how to think. We have to help fill the gaps technology is creating, believing wholeheartedly that parents can make a difference. Technology may be here to stay, but so are parents; both play a major role in our teens' lives.

If you don't know where to start with tackling technology, Dr. Kathy Koch will give you the direction you need. At our Hearts at Home conferences, her workshops are standing room only. She has dedicated her life to understanding kids and helping their parents do the same. *Screens and Teens* will give you hope—and hope is the fuel that keeps parents going.

You can connect with your teens in a wireless world.

JILL SAVAGE
Mother of five
Founder and CEO of Hearts at Home

1

TECHNOLOGY AND OUR DEEPEST HUMAN NEEDS

Most teens today have seen electric typewriters only in the movies (*old* movies or retro movies set in old times), and they may never have seen a manual typewriter. But I'm old enough to remember my family's first typewriters, manual and electric. That big, heavy, gray-and-white piece of technology was a sleek and shiny gift. I loved the changes it brought! Fast typing, with just a light tap on the keys. Tapping a return key instead of lugging across a heavy carriage. Adjusting to that piece of technology was, oh, so worth it!

We've come a long way, haven't we? Now we carry tiny computers in our pockets and purses. We add and delete and access a world of information with just a click or two. The changes—from electric typewriters to today's slim and efficient technological tools—have been continuous. It's the speed of changes that takes my breath away! Change happens now faster than it ever has before.

Is the speed of change influencing our kids? Could that be one of the reasons they're quickly dissatisfied with doing things the same old way? Is this why they want to line up at a store at midnight when a new game, movie, or device hits the market? Is it why they insist we get them the latest and greatest phone or other device even though theirs works just fine?

Our world changes, almost daily, with the changes in technology. And that's innocent, right? It seems as innocent as leaving behind Wite-out to correct typing errors in favor of the laptop's delete key! But are those changes having an impact on our children's behavior and beliefs—and on our own? Yes! In both negative and positive ways, technology with its rapid-fire advances is definitely shaping the personality and character and life path of young people.

> **Parents and teens** are both affected by the influences of our screen-saturated lives, but young people experience the effects with ferocious intensity.

Teens have always experienced peer pressure, but keeping up has reached intense levels of pressure for today's teens, who definitely feel a sense of urgency, as if they're going to be left out unless they have the best, the newest, the fastest, and the easiest.

There's pressure to be the happiest, the most beautiful, the most talented. Do you hear any of these sentiments or see any of these attitudes in your home?

> "My picture got more 'likes' last night than anybody else's. I knew it would."
> "I'm not being rude. I'm multitasking, and I'm good at it."
> "They can't expect me to use that. It's so slow! I've got to buy what Alicia has."
> "That is way too hard. Is there an app to make it easier?"
> "My parents are making such a big deal out of everything! All I'm doing is texting!"
> "This stuff they're making us read is so ridiculous! That book is so old!"

If you haven't heard statements like these in your home yet, give it a minute. You probably will! These attitudes surface repeatedly in our technology-driven world. Listen and watch to see who your teens' "Joneses" may be—those other teens they want so much to keep up with—and consider how much pressure your kids are putting on themselves. While you're at it, pay attention to the pressure influencing you, too.

Our kids live in a world of screens. They have

- Digital/Smart Devices
- Internet/World Wide Web

- Social Networking
- Games, and
- TV/Movies/Radio/Streaming Services

This book isn't really about technology. But it is about how technology influences the beliefs and behaviors of teens and how parents can connect with their children to influence them positively. Parents and teens are both affected by the influences of our screen-saturated lives, but young people experience the effects with ferocious intensity.

I see the signs of screen-world stress in myself—and I'm middle-aged. Perhaps I notice it most in my own impatience (Why did that light just turn red?!) or in my desire to win every game of solitaire I play (I admit it!). I can get annoyed if I forget to program my DVR. I'm grateful for all the music I can choose from—though sometimes I feel so overwhelmed by the numerous choices that I choose nothing at all. I depend on the convenience of the Internet for research, but I also feel frustrated because there's so much information there.

Screens are part of our lives, and they're here to stay. But we long for deep connection with the teens we love. And that means making sure we give our relationships their rightful priority and connect face-to-face.

Being honest and recognizing how technology influences you can improve your relationship with your teens. You can talk about what you have in common rather than being frustrated by differences.

One expert in the effects of media and technology on culture says, technology "is fast, cheap, effective, and cool. That's the good part. The bad part is that it's fast, cheap, effective, and cool."[1] We all know that digital technology itself isn't the problem. Technologies and how we use them can be wonderfully life-giving. They are both tools and toys—tools we need and toys we enjoy. But the content and use of technology can cause problems when they begin to encroach on our development in five core areas of need that both parents and teens share.

TECHNOLOGY AND OUR FIVE CORE NEEDS

My interest in technology took a big leap when my staff and I met with Scott Degraffenreid, a social network analyst and statistician. Scott came to help us understand how young people were being affected by our digital culture and its rapid-fire changes. Scott became a trusted friend and a mentor for me in this area of digital influences.

As a staff we began to apply Scott's information about the culture of technology to what we knew about young people's core needs of *security, identity, belonging, purpose,* and *competence.* Suddenly, the behaviors and problems we'd been recently observing in teens began to make sense.

God created every single person with deep core needs of *security, identity, belonging, purpose,* and *competence.* For more than twenty-five years, I've been teaching about these God-given needs and how, ideally, we meet them in healthy ways. There have always been problems when people try to meet these five core needs in unhealthy or counterfeit ways. I began to see that teens were turning to technology and the digital culture to meet their deep core needs—and technology is a definite counterfeit that doesn't work to meet those needs.

We can start by getting better acquainted with the five core needs. You will find them familiar because you have them yourself!

Security

Security is our first core need, and it's defined by the question *Who can I trust?* We're healthiest when we meet our need for security in God, Jesus, and the Holy Spirit,[2] in trustworthy people, and in ourselves as we learn to be right and do right even when the burden is heavy. Security is rooted in forgiveness—from God, from others, and especially from ourselves.

Technology is not how God designed the need for security to be met.

Everybody has this core need for security; it only becomes a problem when we begin looking for security in all the wrong places. Some young people try to meet their need for security in their technology and its availability. Many believe technology will never let them down (as human relationships often do!).

Perhaps we trust in technology because our computer disasters usually aren't disasters at all. Click a key to "Undo" the keystroke that was a mistake. Power down and reboot, and you're good to go. Have you been with teenagers who are "suffering through" power outages or coping with being at Grandma's house, where the cell signal is weak? Such interruptions of digital connectedness are big deals to them no matter how often we say they shouldn't be. When teens don't have instant access to their technology, their security feels threatened.

Many of today's teens are secure in things being quick, perfect, and easy. They trust that the access they need will always be readily available. They don't need directions to get anywhere because they have a phone with a GPS app. They don't need to remember a friend's phone number because every number is stored in their phones. They don't need to know Bible verses; they can easily look them up on a Bible app, too.

Teens are also secure in their ability to win and to be happy. It's *what* they trust that matters, not *who*. This is potentially very damaging because technology is not how God designed this need for security to be met.

> **Christian parents** cherish hopes that their teens will ultimately have the need for security met deeply, once and for all, by God.

Trusting people doesn't come naturally to young people partly because they're relating through social media and texting. It's hard to truly know people and develop friendship and discernment skills. They may be attempting to meet this need with the number of "friends" they have. What they don't understand is that security is not found in *quantity* (multiple online connections). It's discovered in *quality* (real and faithful relationships).

Christian parents cherish the hopes that their teens will ultimately have this need for security met deeply, once and for all, by God. But whether teens will rely on God to meet their need for security may be influenced by technology. The Web provides easy access to ideas about many religions and many gods. Some teens follow people we don't know through services like Twitter. They can access information without us being aware. Information could be presented to them (without their looking for it!) via advertising or links in their social feeds. People they follow and sites they visit may report things about the God of the Bible and the way we're choosing to raise our children that might cause them to think we're wrong and our God isn't the only One worth worshiping.

What is worship, after all? It's assigning lordship to God and giving him our attention and praise—and giving him primacy in our days.[3] Have you ever seen teens with their tech tools and wondered if they almost worship their technology? It's where they turn for answers to their questions and to solve their problems. Others unwittingly downgrade God, treating Him casually like a friend on Facebook who may or may not like their status update. As teens become increasingly acclimated to speedy answers via the Internet, will it be harder for them to wait on God for an answer to prayer, if they do pray? Will young people be satisfied with a Bible app that provides a devotional each morning, considering that bit of Scripture as all the spiritual nourishment they need?

You can immediately realize that there are spiritual implications that accompany deep involvement with screens! But it's not all doom and gloom. A young person's security grows as they become more self-confident. Gaining knowledge (by using tech tools and platforms) can grow that "self-security." The ease of Facebook, Instagram, Twitter, and texting reinforces and can even strengthen relationships as they allow teens to be in regular contact and share much about their lives. For the discerning user, these platforms can also reveal inconsistencies, manipulation, and pride, clues that the wise young person can use to make better decisions about which friends he or she should keep at a distance and which they should engage with more personally.

Screens can positively affect faith development, too. Bible apps are convenient, and they allow us to keep the Bible with us. Devotional material read on handheld devices and Facebook posts from ministries, churches, and friends can encourage, humble, and mature young people. Worship music and videos of church services and concerts can be inspiring. Streaming allows teens to watch church services and conferences they might have missed in person.

When it comes to meeting our deep human need for security,

we want technology to take its rightful place. Digital tools can't meet anyone's need for security, but they can be tools that help teens develop the relationships with God and others that are real and trustworthy and nourishing.

Identity

Identity is our second core need. It's defined by the question *Who am I?* Because the way we define ourselves influences our behavior, it's essential that our identity is current and honest. This means we see ourselves accurately. Ignoring our weak areas or challenges is immature. Denying our strengths is just as bad. It's important for us to know who we are!

For some teens, screen use has contributed to an under-developed identity. They may be devoting so much time to gaming and staying connected with "friends" that they don't have time or desire to broaden their interests or learn new skills, which would grow and solidify their identity. Also, because technology makes many things easier, they may be lacking the perseverance, diligence, and teachability that are often essential for adding to their skill sets and character development. Posting on social networks can limit identity development because the tendency is for posts to acknowledge only certain aspects of their lives. That means friends and family can only provide comments or ask questions about those elements—the ones the teens choose to show. For example, they may post often about their musical interests and never mention that they volunteer at an animal shelter.

As time goes by and no friends acknowledge or support the teen's interest in animal rescue, the teen may begin to devalue that interest and let it wane.

When young people interact with many people on social media platforms, their identity can get confused. Many of the people whose posts they follow don't even know them personally. Those writers are just making general statements about their generation. Yet their words can be very influential.

Words—even words tossed off casually on a social media venue—can strongly affect our teens. If someone whose opinion your daughter values makes a disparaging comment about her writing, she may dismiss her writing ability as unimportant. If she likes a particular sports team but finds out very few other people do, she may decide her inclination was wrong. In a matter of minutes, she can transition from believing one thing about herself to another. This shift in identity negatively influences security because she appears to be inconsistent.

Your son may "like" a musical group one day, and being a fan becomes part of his identity. After he finds out someone he values doesn't like that group, he'll quickly "unlike" them. But what about his friends who were glad he liked that group? Now they're confused and may communicate that to your son. They might actually be disappointed or angry. Now your son will experience the stress associated with trying to keep everyone happy.

But is this really so different from when we were teens ourselves? After all, we listened to the opinions of our peers—or of

Today's young people tend to be more conflicted about who they are and what they value.

celebrities we read about or saw on television. The vast difference lies in quantity! Today's young people are coping with a deluge of widely divergent influences, while we had a much smaller circle of people influencing us, and they were probably more unified in their preferences. And the influence is nearly constant! Before there were cellphones, young people had time off from their peers—times when they were at home with just their families. Now teens are with their peers and with online influences 24/7 since they can access their social media and the Internet all day long.

Because of this large array of influences in their daily experience, today's young people tend to be more conflicted about who they are and what they value. It's even harder for parents to know their kids well—and for teens to benefit from the opinions and wisdom of the parents who love them because they're listening to so many voices.

But before we overreact and unplug all of our screens, let's remember that technology can also enhance a teen's identity. Today's cameras allow young people to easily record and express what they enjoy and what they do. They can share through social media and gain interest and support from family and friends. Also, posts from others may inspire them to consider fresh ideas and undertake new projects or adventures. Teens can follow through where their personal interests lead them because finding information through the Web is easy.

Christian parents know that young people will be most whole and healthy when their identities are grounded in their relationship with God. The Bible is where they found out that they are created in God's image (Genesis 1:27), deeply loved (1 John 4:10), bought with a price (1 Corinthians 7:23), and so much more. Ideally they will add to these truths the pursuit of a personal relationship with Christ. Teens' use of the Internet and other tech tools can cause them to believe Christian truths or not. It depends on what websites they peruse, who they follow and listen to, how they use social media, and the types of television shows and movies they watch.

Belonging

Belonging is the third core need, and it's defined by the question *Who wants me?* Belonging is healthiest when we meet this need by belonging to God,[4] with people who have demonstrated solid character, and among people with whom we share beliefs, interests, and/or talents. Unique connections and belonging can also be found through differences because new experiences can bond us.

Belonging is dependent upon our security and identity. When one or both of these needs aren't met or they're met in illegitimate ways, we either won't experience belonging at all or our belonging will be unhealthy. For example, teens who place their security in technology are more likely also to attempt to meet their belonging need through technology. They prioritize time with technology over time with people. Their digital relationships will be most significant to them.

Some teens stay busy with their technology, which can make investing in person-to-person friendships difficult. Also, social media tends to promote a lack of authenticity and accountability. A cut-and-run reaction to negativity is common and results in short-lived relationships. Using this same response with face-to-face friendships is damaging to the feelings and belonging of all parties involved.

As we remember technology isn't good or bad, but the use of it can be either, we must recognize that platforms like Instagram and Facebook can enhance relationships. Although I have many "friends" on Facebook I don't even know, some people who started as friends of friends or women who heard me speak somewhere have become women I'd like to get to know better in person. Young adults and teens can also spark new friendships through social media. This might be especially true for teens with social anxiety and those who are introverted or self-smart. We, of course, need to be alert regarding their online connections.

Simple games on phones can strengthen relationships. My own sister-in-law has enjoyed an ongoing competition with my niece's fiancé. It wouldn't be healthy if they related to each other only through this game, but their friendship has grown from sharing this game. Playing the game was fun and increased their comfort with each other. It gave them something to talk about when they were together in person.

Posting pictures can enhance relationships. This week my niece and my cousin's daughter both posted old family pictures to commemorate an event. Soon lots of family members were chiming in with comments. For those few moments, our family didn't feel so separated geographically.

How might technology help teens discover and strengthen their belonging to God and to their church families? We've mentioned how teens can access the Bible through apps. This can make the study and memorization of Scripture easier and more likely. Young people might enjoy keeping up with posts from a church or youth group Facebook page or Instagram account. Many church youth groups pull students from various schools (public, private, homeschool), so social media groups might give teens a natural way to stay connected on the weekdays when they are not together for Sunday school classes or youth meetings.

The flip side of the coin is that screen-time influences can weaken a young person's belonging in their families or in their churches or to God. Screen time can occupy a lot of hours in a teen's day, keeping him or her busier than we'd like. Time with games and videos and social media platforms leaves less time for Christian peers, for attending church and youth group functions, and for reading the Bible. The pattern of quickly dipping in and out of social media creates a pattern of relating that doesn't work well when it comes to relating to God in a meaningful way. And teens' impatience with anything less than a rapid response is exacerbated by constant media use; it makes waiting on God's answers in their lives seem interminable.

If these concepts sound familiar, it's because our need for belonging is so closely linked to our need for security. We long for our young people to have this pair of deep needs fully met through healthy relationships.

Today's teens are multitalented and multipassionate.

Purpose

Purpose is our fourth core need; it's defined by the question *Why am I alive?* The A+ answer is that we're alive to glorify God through who we are and what we do.[5] We need to know and develop our strengths, strengthen weaknesses, and accept challenges that are a part of who we are.

Because today's teens are multitalented and often multipassionate, they need direction in order to discover and believe in their specific purpose. Finding personal purpose is one of the great challenges of life. There's so much information available for teens to sift through, and they know they have many options during high school and beyond. Sometimes having so many choices before them has a demobilizing effect; they're like deer caught in the glare of headlights! Young people have a lot of sifting and sorting of their ideas and talents and passions to get through, and that can feel overwhelming. Also, if some of the other core needs aren't met, it can warp the way young people approach finding their purpose. For example, if a teen's security and identity are wrapped up in being happy, she will choose only activities that keep her happy and may avoid opportunities that stretch her. She might bypass substantive factors that could shape her future.

One of the keys to finding purpose is hope. Hope gives rise to purpose. Social media can give young people exposure to fresh ideas and the great, big world out there. The Internet offers places where teens may discover causes they care about and people to follow who are doing good work. A broad security, complete and accurate identity, and people to connect and serve with will help youth do more than just "like" organizations. At the same time, the negativity and bullying that take place on many social media platforms can rob teens of their hope. The constant barrage of causes and themes can also have a numbing effect; teens get used to hitting "Like" and then moving on. That level of low commitment is all too common online. Again, technology gives and technology takes away.

Young people with a healthy purpose will come into their adult lives with a readiness to engage the world around them. Parents long to see young people find purpose in real-world pursuits and passions.

Competence

Competence is the fifth core need, and it's defined by the question *What do I do well?* We'll believe we have competence and can develop more when we have trustworthy people speaking into our lives (security). Furthermore, our competence is related to who we are (identity), it's often discovered as we commit to others (belonging), and it's found in God so we can fulfill our unique purpose.[6] Purpose makes competence necessary. Without it, we don't need to be good at anything.

> **God didn't** wire us to need perfection, but he did wire us for competence.

God didn't wire us to need perfection, but he did wire us for competence—the ability to do what we need to do. If we're striving for perfection, that's not a desire from God. It may mean we're prideful, uncomfortable with our weaknesses, and not trusting God's grace. Young people can struggle to believe in their competence because of how easy it is to base our worth and ability on how we compare to others on social media platforms. We can always find someone more beautiful and more able there.

So, short of striving for perfection, where do teens develop competence? To incorporate a couple of clichés, young people need to "stretch their wings" and "test their mettle." They need to tackle adventures that make them a bit nervous because they've never done those things before. This is how they find out where they're weak and might need to get stronger. This is how their strengths are affirmed. All of these experiences produce strong competence.

While they're discovering their personal giftedness or limitations, they are exercising a faith muscle—trusting God in new challenges and new relationships and learning how to seek His wisdom and empowerment.

The Bible promises that when we are weak, He is strong and His grace is sufficient (2 Corinthians 12:9–10). When we find it hard to love, His love for us allows love to grow (1 John 4:7). Because of our faith in God through Christ, we can do all things (Philippians 4:13). Just as a connection with God enables the meeting of the other four core needs, that relationship makes competence possible as well.

MEETING CORE NEEDS IN THE BEST WAYS

Along with their parents, teens have five core needs—for security, identity, belonging, purpose, and competence. Technology offers some good tools for meeting these five needs, but if we aren't mindful and observant, those tools can get in the way of meeting those needs. That's why young people need training in discernment when it comes to their digital choices. Bringing wise influence to bear in this area must be a major parenting goal.

Influencing our teens regarding technology is going to hinge on a lot of communication-discussions about their choices and ours, sharing the reasons for the choices we make, listening to one another with affection and respect. We need to understand our teens and their digital world better and understand the way a teen's mind works. Parents can grow in confidence and skills for parenting young people in a digital age. You may catch this vision for your role in your teen's development in the pages ahead.[7]

"I have the right to do anything," you say—
but not everything is beneficial. "I have the right
to do anything"—but not everything is constructive.

1 Corinthians 10:23

Finally, brothers and sisters, whatever is true, whatever is
noble, whatever is right, whatever is pure, whatever is lovely,
whatever is admirable—if anything is excellent or
praiseworthy—think about such things.

Philippians 4:8

2

TRUTHS ABOUT
TODAY'S TEENS

Arriving at Purdue University as a freshman and getting to know other students, I was able to connect with many other students. It was clear we had much in common even though we lived throughout the United States and in other countries, too. Some of us ordered "pop" while others ordered "soda," and some of us thought the others had an accent when they spoke. But for the most part, my generation had a strong set of similar expectations, beliefs, goals, and experiences. Most of us were there to study, and most of us enjoyed the competitive athletics and rivalries between colleges. It didn't matter what dorm someone lived in, similar music could be heard coming from different rooms.

Fast-forward a generation or two. A generation spans about twenty years—from birth to young adulthood. Those in the Millennial generation were born from 1982 to 2002. During those years the personal computer was invented and the Internet was launched. In that same era, cable television became widely available, video games were more affordable, and the first crude brick-sized cellphones became available. If you're thirty-two or younger, you've never known life without technology. You've incorporated it as naturally as those of us who are older incorporated turning pages while reading books and changing television channels by getting up and physically rotating the dial.

Young people don't think about their technology. Some use the analogy that it's like breathing air. They just do it. Alan Kay, a visionary computer scientist, declared, "Technology is technology only for people who are born before it was invented."[1]

Those of us who've been around for these decades of rapid change have accommodated to technology. We've made adjustments to add it to our lives. We've learned to Google search and download and email and surf the Net and finger swipe to turn digital pages. At first we had to think about what we were doing—and now these actions are beginning to be reflexive.

Technology has transformed communication—and it's changing our brains.

Some of us are more motivated to accommodate our lives to technology than others. My brother and I were so proud of our mom many years ago, when, at the age of seventy-two, she chose to learn how to use email and websites. It was a huge adjustment for Mom, who was content with her landline and encyclopedias. But she found purpose to motivate her: My brother and I both traveled internationally and she wanted to stay in touch with us.

Whether technology is something you've always known or something you've adapted to, there's no denying that technology has transformed communication. It's also changing our brains.

CULTURE CULTIVATES THE BRAIN

For proof that God is generous, we don't need to look any further than our brains. He created us with 100 billion neurons, cells that are the brain's conduits of information. At the time of birth, each of these is connected to other neurons an average of five thousand times for a total number of fifty trillion connections. (That's a fifty followed by twelve zeroes!) By the time children are three, the number of connections has expanded twenty times, to a thousand trillion.[2]

It's those connections between the neurons that cause us to think the way we do. Only about 20 percent of those connections are hardwired by God.[3] They account for things we all learn. If our brains are functioning correctly, we roll over, creep, crawl, walk, and run. Listen and talk. See, smell, and taste. Scribble and then write legibly.

Connections of the other 80 percent of the brain's neurons are formed by what we do prior to age twenty-five.[4] Doing something a few times won't result in a firm connection, but repetitive beliefs, attitudes, and actions result in solid connections. They are considered "soft" in comparison to the hardwiring God causes during conception, but they become "harder" the more we use them. I'm thankful we can still learn new things as we age!

My trainer at the gym, Linda, gets this concept. She recently put me on machine I hadn't used in quite a while, with a higher weight. During the first set I completed, the lift was very challenging. During the second and third sets, it was much easier. It wasn't that I was miraculously stronger in the ten minutes between sets. My muscles just remembered lifting the weight.

Just as my muscles have expectations, my brain expects to do the things it often does. It remembers what it's done before. That's why patterns can be challenging to break. Attitudes, reactions, and actions we often have are the ones we'll have again.

The gym where I work out added a back room—with especially challenging equipment in it. The activities Linda has me do back there are tough! For a while when that back room was still a novelty, Linda would say, "Let's head to the back." And I'd moan or joke, "Let's not!" But then I recognized that my negativity was influencing my efforts. My brain was expecting me not to be happy! So I adopted a new strategy and intentionally stopped verbalizing my displeasure, even as a joke. Instead, I focused on my improvements.

So what influences the brain patterns of today's teens? Whatever they experience often is going to influence their beliefs and their behaviors. And guess what they're experiencing often? Everything tech.

Have you identified some specific concerns about your teens? Is it their impatience? Their multitasking that you interpret as rude? Entitlement attitudes? Not enough sleep? Complaining? Academic apathy? Quick boredom? Believe it or not, it's not their fault they are that way.

Of course your teens have a responsibility to honor and respect you and other authority figures in their lives. But the reality is that the various screens and different devices they use have caused them to believe what they believe and behave how they behave. We'd be no different if we were their age. Okay, I'm just going to make you read that again: We'd be no different if we were their age! We'd have been trained up on the same daily tech exposure and would be struggling with the same belief and behavior issues.

Take an honest look at yourself. Are any of the impatience, multitasking, sleeplessness, complaining, entitlement, apathy, or boredom issues more present in your own life than they were five years ago? Or even a year ago? I have to be truthful: They are for me. Even as adults we continue to be influenced by what we see, hear, and do.

God is able to transform our minds.

But our brain patterns—and our thinking minds—can be transformed in good ways as well. It's one of the ways God is good to us: He is able to transform our minds.[5]

Nurture

Two things shape a generation. One is the nurture it receives during the developmental years. Technology tools and toys have the largest influence on brain development of today's teens and children because they spend so much time with these devices. While they're passively viewing or actively interacting with their screens, neurons are being connected in certain ways. Because those of us who are older had different experiences when we were young, our brains are biologically wired differently. Our different neural pathways mean our brains process and execute differently. That's one of the reasons generational dynamics can be challenging. We have an actual technology generation gap!

Children who are consistently handed phones or tablets by parents who want to keep them busy are being nurtured more by technology than by their own parents. Often, even when parents are engaged with their kids, technology is still ever-present. What attracts more of teen's attention? It's what or who is doing the nurturing. For some young people, technology is present in the home *and* in the culture at large. For others, it might be present more in the larger culture, but technology and its influence can't be ignored even then. Those of us who are older were raised *with* technology, but many of today's young people are being raised *by* technology.

Today's young people are being raised by technology.

Challenges during Developmental Years

The second influence on a generation's formation is the challenges it faces. Technology influences these, too. Our teens haven't had nearly the number of personal challenges those of us who are older have had because technology has made things easier. But it's also made them more aware of worldwide struggles and complexities than any generation before.

My parents told my brother and me about how they'd go to the movies on Saturday and watch news stories with war footage in the theater before the featured film began. That war footage was heavily edited, and it was already fairly dated by the time anyone saw it. When I was young, my brother and I watched television newscasts with war footage. That was also carefully edited. But today's young adults, teens, and children are exposed early and often to real-time, raw, unedited footage of wars and crises from all over the world. And they don't just see it, they hear it too. The sounds of war, school shootings, and homelessness are also real to them.

When I was young, I heard about starving children and might have seen occasional photographs. Today we can see these children in television commercials, during news reports, on documentaries, and even in social media ads in various sidebars across the Internet. Now it's not just those from emerging nations, but hungry, homeless, and ill children from America stare back at us from screens. Our children and teens see them, too—up close and personal on the screens in their homes or in their hands.

While there are generational generalities, we must not paint all teens with one broad stroke. Although nurture and challenges are primary influencers, other things contribute to make young people who they are. For this reason, not everything we cover in these pages will be 100 percent applicable for 100 percent of your teens and children. Things like education, personality, learning styles, passions, and spiritual gifts also contribute to make our teens who they are. Family values and faith are also major influencers on how they develop. Whether children have personal faith in Christ and are being led into maturity in Christ may be the most important factor when it comes to not allowing the negative potential of screens to change them. Understanding some key truths about our kids will help us.

FIVE KEY TRUTHS ABOUT TEENS

A large portion of this book is going to be about debunking the lies that come to our teens because of our technology-saturated culture, but for now we get to focus on some *truths*. I offer five essential insights that help us understand teens' beliefs, motivations, choices, and behaviors.

Truth #1: Teens' Relationships Cause Beliefs

Jordan's family had relocated, and they were trying to find a new church. His parents insisted he attend a youth group activity on a Friday night. He wasn't there long when he texted his mom: "Come get me, please. Nobody here knows me, and I don't know them!"

Being in a situation without established relationships was stressing him out because Jordan's identity is closely tied to his relationships. In between churches, Jordan no longer felt like himself. He didn't really know who he was anymore!

Young people prioritize relationships. Notice, I didn't write that they prioritize friendships or people. No. They prioritize relationships. Some relationships are strong—usually with people they know and spend time with face-to-face. Others are with people they know but spend little if any time with. Then there are relationships with people on social media who they may not know at all. This can include friends of friends. It can include Hollywood actors they find fascinating who they read about on websites and follow on Twitter and Instagram. The relationships may be with musicians, designers of their favorite games or apps, politicians, or even pastors.

Teens have relationship-based beliefs. Adults usually have belief-based relationships.

Because they value relationships and want to keep people happy, they have *relationship-based beliefs*. Since teens tend to base their opinions and beliefs on what other people think, they may not be able to defend their views well initially. In fact, the views are really not *their* views—at least not deeply. Teens downplay and even ignore experts and people in authority over them when making decisions and choices. Rather, they rely on who they know (or who they *think* they know). These "friends" influence their beliefs and, therefore, their behaviors. This is why young people change their minds often. They listen to different people with different ideas and decide to agree with them. This can be frustrating for parents, teachers, and pastors who thought a teen's mind was made up. It probably was, but not for long.

Those of us who are older usually don't change our beliefs as often as teens do. Our beliefs have become the starting point for relationships and not the other way around. We know what we believe and choose to relate most intimately with people who have similar beliefs. Because we decide and control what influences we allow in our lives, we are less likely to change our minds. It's not that we're unteachable. But we value our beliefs and won't compromise them just because someone thinks we should. We have *belief-based relationships.*

That changeability for teens has its upside! The good news is, with relationship-based beliefs, when teens adopt a belief we disapprove of, it may be easier to get them to change their minds. But, of course, that happens most as they truly believe we want to be in relationship with them. Teens are influenced by relationship—and so parents have to grow the relationship. We have to show them we believe our relationship is meaningful so that they believe the relationship is meaningful. It doesn't matter what we *say* is true. It's what teens *see* as true.

One parent shared that when she and her son were going through a tough time, he wrote her a note about his frustrations.

Among other things he communicated, "I don't know you. And I feel you don't know me. You talk to me about things that need to be done around the house but you don't talk to me about my thoughts or feelings about stuff." His words were a wake-up call for her to invest more intentionally in a meaningful relationship with her son.

Be alert for teachable moments and relevant times to share about your life as you listen to stories about theirs. You know the wrong timing will quickly kill their interest. Don't give up! Through shared stories, differences and similarities will become clear. That's a good basis for conversations, and two-way communication will build deeper and more honest relationships.

You can build your relationship with your teen by keeping an open mind about his or her network of relationships. Don't constantly dismiss the people they relate to. Try to cultivate your awareness of who is in your teen's life.

If you have trouble getting your teen to open up so your relationship can be more authentic, try writing notes back and forth. You can do this at night or leave a note on your teen's bed while he or she is at school. Teens tell me they like collecting their thoughts without emotions getting in the way when responding to questions or concerns you bring up. They tell me they can feel ambushed when a parent calls, "Come here. We need to talk." If they haven't been aware there's a problem, they're not ready to discuss it—and the parent has a great advantage during the conversation. Writing gives both parents and teens the chance to consider their responses.

Whether you work side by side, take your teen out for a coke, or use a pillow journal, it's important to invest in your relationship with them. Their beliefs are heavily influenced by their relationships. Make sure you're one of those influential relationships.

Truth #2: Teens Want to Improve the World

Because teens have seen many hardships, tragedies, and hurt in our broken world via the World Wide Web, many are energized to solve problems. They want to improve something that's wrong. Some care about kids across the world from them (even if they may not notice the kids in their church or school). Other teens care for those they know and seem disinterested in the needs of those they don't know in person. Big or small, young people see their efforts as creating a better world. This stereotypical wide-eyed idealization seems to be a rite of passage that is further magnified by the stimuli provided online.

Teens' motivations also differ. Some genuinely care about people. Some just care about proving they can do something big. Some want attention and recognition for what they do. This may be the case if they watch certain reality television shows and have seen peers gain position and popularity because of their good acts. A teen's own self-centered tendencies can also be a factor, but parents can have huge influence here.

A friend of mine has gotten to know a group of homeless people in Chicago. She regularly takes them backpacks full of supplies and food. Her children help her collect what they need, pack the backpacks, write personal notes, pray for them, and sometimes deliver the food and supplies with her. My friend and her kids love these people. These children, and others raised like them, will more likely serve to help rather than because it makes them look good.

When I posted a question about today's teens on Facebook, this response reflected the common theme: "What I appreciate most about the teenagers I work with is their desire and drive to take action. They don't want to just talk about the problems that exist in our culture, they want to be a driving force behind creating new culture." What a great trait for a generation of young people to embody!

Another response read, "Most of them truly want to make the world a better place. If you give them a 'purpose' they are full-steam-ahead. We joke that if we said our church was a church plant we would have college kids coming out our ears. They want to be a part of something that 'means' something to the world."

Because of this awareness of the problems of the world, some teens get overwhelmed by all that's wrong. These young people may believe they can't do enough so they choose to do nothing. It may be because they don't know their strengths or how their strengths are relevant to the issue at hand. They may be prone to depression. Is it surprising that parents whose talk is negative and pessimistic tend to raise children not oriented to change?

This paralysis and inaction can also occur when parents appear overwhelmed. Frankly, being overwhelmed is understandable.

News reports are all around us. Apps and email blasts keep us informed. Media decision-makers who determine what is news-worthy almost always choose bad news. Crawls on websites and televisions announce bad weather, bad traffic, and bad anything else.

This desire to improve the world, which is a strength, can contribute to apathy at church and at school. If teens don't believe the content being taught by authority figures or talking heads will help them improve the world the way they want to, deep down, they may not engage. This apathy can lead to disrespect for authority, sporadic attendance, low grades, and an increase in the dropout rate.

Our young people want to change the world.

Our young people want to change the world. They see authority figures, world problems, and even the daily news through this filter. Helping them identify opportunities and then learn to serve is one way we can influence this truth in the right direction. As they serve in small ways, they learn that their efforts can make a difference in the world.

Truth #3: Teens Are Creative, Innovative, and Entrepreneurial

Have you noticed your teens coming up with new and different approaches to ordinary tasks? Have they suggested unique solutions for dysfunction they're aware of in their community or elsewhere in the world? Their creative and innovative spirits are birthed in their desire to solve problems and their exposure to many different ideas on websites, blogs, videos, and elsewhere. Many are also entrepreneurial, especially turning these ideas into nonprofits and personalized volunteer opportunities. As film director Justin Dillon said, "It used to be the coolest thing you could do when you were a teenager is start a band. Now the coolest thing you can do is start a nonprofit."[6]

How can we take advantage of these abilities and increase our teens' motivation? When discussing current issues and things that matter to our young people, we can consider how they naturally think and ask them, "What might be a better way to do this?" Help them put their creative gifts to the test! Making it easy for teens to bring up new ideas honors them and their unique contributions.

Realize teens may get bored quickly and frustrated easily when expected to do things the same way all the time. They may also get frustrated when their ideas are constantly rejected. Of course, they need to learn how to communicate their ideas and ask questions with respectful attitudes. Otherwise, they may be appropriately judged as critical, arrogant, and prideful.

Teens have always been bright and have always had something to offer. But this generation seems uniquely aware of big problems and uniquely motivated to tackle them! Asking for their ideas and encouraging them to think is an important strategy in embracing their creative, innovative, and entrepreneurial spirit.

Truth #4: Their Security Is in Technology

I speak to a lot of parent groups. When I ask parents of teens to indicate if they're frustrated by how hard it is to get their kids to turn off their phones, stop listening to their music, and power down their screens, virtually every hand goes up. It's one of parenting's most consistent frustrations. And then I ask the parents if it's hard for them to turn off their own devices. Nervous laughter and looks around the room follow.

Today's young people are known to say, "You might as well cut off my arm if you're going to take away my phone." Technology is like breathing to the average teen. It's a normal, everyday part of life they don't even think about. A contemporary cartoonist might show a child clutching a phone instead of a security blanket. Teens associate comfort with access to technology.

Let's be honest: It's not their fault screens are teens' security. They've been raised with technology; their brains are wired to use and depend on these technological tools. It started young for them! Think about it: How many of us adults have handed even young children a handheld device to entertain and even soothe them?

But I'll say it again: No "thing" will ever meet young people's legitimate need for security. They should find it in us, in others who are worthy of their trust, and in themselves when they have a healthy self-awareness and behave wisely. Most importantly, they should learn to place their security in God. But the reality is that technology is often a teenager's security.

Truth #5: They're Tech-Addicted, Tired, Stressed, Overwhelmed, Depressed, and Escaping

If you've observed any of these emotional states in the teens and children you love, you're not alone. The problems you've observed may be why you picked up this book in the first place. It's hard to connect in healthy ways with anyone who is tech-addicted, tired, depressed, stressed, over-

> **The technology** is not as perfect or as nurturing as our teens need it to be.

whelmed, and/or lonely. This is especially true for teens, who don't have as many coping strategies as adults. If you haven't observed these consistently in your children, thank God! But talk with your teens, and you'll find that many of their friends are struggling with tech addiction, fatigue, stress, feeling overwhelmed, depression, and escapism.

Where do all these issues stem from? The technology is not as perfect or as nurturing as our teens need it to be. The messages they've pulled from vast doses of screen time have been hugely influential, and they send widely varied messages. All that conflicting data is stressful; our teens' subconscious beliefs may be very conflicted. And the less-than-real presentation of images on a screen can establish some disconnect with teens' reality. Why isn't their world as cool, as clever, as beautiful as the one they see on screen? Why aren't they similarly cool, clever, and beautiful?

Parents have the unique role of being able to provide

truth-training for their teens. We can provide feedback about who our teens really are. Our accurate assessment of their personal worth can help them not to be so hard on themselves. We can help them assess the limitations of technology.

To increase our understanding, let's look at the dynamics of each of the elements in Truth #5.

Tech Addiction. Habits are things we choose to do repeatedly. They can either be healthy and wise or unhealthy and unwise. If you start paying attention to your habits, you'll find they usually fall into one of two categories: good and bad. If a bad habit drives our behavior, we can, with some intentionality, choose to stop it in time. Of course, our good habits, like praying with our children, playing with them, and patiently answering their questions, are habits we don't want to stop!

Not every teen who uses lots of technology is addicted. Some have simply developed habits like playing certain games, using websites to learn about actors in their favorite movies, and texting among friends. On the other hand, when behavior is driven by an addiction, we are "unable to control the aspects of the addiction without help because of the mental or physical conditions involved."[7]

Almost four in ten young people fear they are addicted to the Internet.[8] One twelve-year-old girl reports, "The Internet nearly always controls my actions. I have been told that I am addicted to the Internet, and prefer its company rather than being with other people. I feel lost without the Internet."[9] Because of the dangers of addiction, we must be alert to our children's use of technology and their attitudes and behaviors when they're not connected. Addiction can trigger other negatives like fatigue, depression, anxiety, and loneliness.[10]

In the face of these factors, parents still have great influence over our teens. Not only do they watch how we cope with frustrations, boredom, and impatience, they also watch how we use technology. If parents disengage from children to stare at screens, children will likely do the same.

Because of what we know about how the brain's soft-wiring develops, we must be diligent. The National Center on Addiction and Substance Abuse at Columbia University tells us why addiction is more prevalent during formative years than it is for adults: "Because the teen brain is still developing, addictive substances physically alter its structure and function faster and more intensely than in adults, interfering with brain development, further impairing judgment and heightening the risk of addiction."[11]

Children who develop addictions to screens are much more susceptible to developing other addictions someday. Research suggests 90 percent of addictions have roots in the teen years. To further drive home this point, one in four Americans who began using any addictive substance before age eighteen are addicted, compared to one in twenty-five who started using at age twenty-one or older.[12]

A little illustration may paint a picture of what happens in the brain with addiction. We're in the middle of a serious drought where I live so our rivers have less water than normal. Some have dried up completely. Yet the river's banks are still there. I can still see where the water belongs. When it rains, that's where the water will flow. The banks will once again serve their purpose.

Patterns in the brain form because repetition much like water forces a pattern into the dirt when the river is first formed. When the same things (good or bad) are done over time, it's easy for us to keep doing them. Just like the water can't control where it goes, we may feel like we can't control our fingers or minds and where they go. A pattern has been set that can be hard to change. It becomes routine, a new normal. Habits, if we're not careful, become addiction. When you're playing a game on your computer, have you ever intended to click on "exit" but you clicked on "play again"? Have you reached for your phone so often at red lights that now it's hard not to? Those are habits ingrained into your brain connections.

Just as a river's banks will continue to support and direct the water, the brain's patterns will continue to support our behavior. It's hard not to continue. Change is possible—definitely—but change won't be automatic or even easy. Teens need to see us being transparent about our own negative habits. We can share personal examples of our own history with changing bad habits or reversing negative routine behaviors. We need to show them we're willing to move from recognizing problems to taking action to change our behaviors at the same time we're expecting them to work at changing theirs.

When we limit our use of screens and encourage our teens toward other activities, we're digging new "river banks," so to speak. The new patterns will replace the automatic reach for a screen. Not only will this enrich teens' lives today, it makes it less likely that addictions to drugs, alcohol, eating disorders, cutting, and tobacco may happen in the future.

So play outside, go for walks as a family, attend sporting events, and plant a garden. Play board games as a family and talk and laugh while you play. Read together and discuss what you read. Listen to engaging literature or appropriate sermons or podcasts when in the car. Discuss what you enjoy and find intriguing. Make meals together. Enjoy life, fight tech addiction, and reprogram your family's brain patterns at the same time!

Fatigue. Fatigue can be a very real side effect of too much screen time. Because technology too often distracts them while studying, kids stay up later to get work finished. Also, too many are sleeping with their phones and waking with every incoming text. Others are gaming in the middle of the night. Two-thirds of eleven- to seventeen-year-olds take their tablet, smartphone, or laptop to bed and talk to friends online, play games, and watch films. Only a third does homework on the devices.[13] Our internal light cues and sleep-inducing hormones are influenced by the glowing lights emitted by screens. When the lights are bright, the brain can even be tricked to think it's daytime.[14]

Fatigue is dangerous for many reasons. You know this from your own experience. Would you agree you don't think as carefully or clearly when tired? We're all aware of warnings against driving while overtired. But all of us have experienced that sluggishness of mind that comes with weariness, and most of us have regretted decisions made when we were way too tired. We adults experience these issues even though our brain development is complete. How much more might fatigue be causing thinking problems for our kids whose brains are not yet fully formed?

Teens' grades are negatively affected because of fatigue.[15] When they're tired they have trouble focusing on, organizing, and completing their school work.

In the battle against screen-related fatigue, one strategy might be to require teens to recharge their cellphones overnight in the kitchen or another room that's far from their bedrooms. Your phone company may allow you to use parental controls to set time restrictions over the hours your teens' phones are active. Maybe it would be enough at your house just to set a phones-off time of 9:00 or 10:00 p.m. on school nights. My friend Jill knows a family that changes their Wifi password daily at bedtime. They give their kids the password the next day once they know chores and homework obligations have been fulfilled. Whatever you choose to do, you can take proactive measures to battle fatigue in your teens.

Stressed and overwhelmed. These are common emotional states for teens. Feeling overwhelmed usually causes stress. And feeling overwhelmed can result in emotional and activity shutdown. When there's too much too cope with, teens can develop apathy toward the problems that concern them. Being overwhelmed can muddy their thinking and lead to apathy, depression, and intellectual, emotional, and social paralysis.[16]

Whether or not your teen uses the word *overwhelmed*, the feelings and concept emerge as teens talk about their struggles. They're often overwhelmed by all the information that's available and they're not sure how to process it all. This can lead to failure to make choices —or to making muddled choices instead of consistently wise ones.

It's not just our kids who have to learn to manage information overload.

We may also be overwhelmed. For adults, media-overload is the seventh leading cause of stress.[17] It's not just our kids who have to learn to manage information overload. We have to tackle this, too! What contributes to this? Practically every minute of every day:

- YouTube users upload 48 hours of new video.
- Email users send 204,166,667 messages.
- Google receives over 2,000,000 search queries.
- Facebook users share 684,478 pieces of content.
- Twitter users send over 100,000 tweets.
- Apple receives about 47,000 app downloads.
- Brands and organizations on Facebook receive 34,722 "likes."
- Instagram users share 3,600 new photos.

- 571 new websites are created.
- WordPress users publish 347 new blog posts.[18]

There's never been a better time for having information at our fingertips! Yet the reality of managing the massive amount of information presents challenges previous generations never had to experience. Feeling stressed and overwhelmed is a logical by-product of so much data and so many messages headed our way.

Depressed and escaping. More parents than ever before approach me after seminars to talk about their teens' depression. I hear about kids who used to be involved and outgoing who are now closed off from friends. These parents aren't alone, and you aren't either, if that's part of your story. "In 2013, 29.9 percent of students nationwide had felt so sad or hopeless almost every day for two or more weeks in a row that they stopped doing some usual activities."[19]

Escaping from depression, other feelings, and much of life is a solution for this generation just as it's been for all of us who have gone before. Where in the past sedating pain with alcohol, drugs, and sex were too common, today's teens may be choosing the social scroll (browsing through social media feeds) and music. These very behaviors may feed their addiction and isolation and can result in more of the very thing they're trying to escape.

Are you familiar with the term *couch potato*? It's been used to describe people who sit in front of the television for hours on end. I like to call people who just sit in church without engaging "pew potatoes." Now, due to fatigue, stress, boredom, and being overwhelmed we can talk in terms of "scroll potatoes." As my co-worker Randy Thomas, our Celebrate Kids online content and social media manager, says, "The feeds of social networks can cause an infinite waste of time as people scroll through their feeds looking for a laugh or distraction."

Suicide is a horrifying form of escape affecting many more young people than most of us realize. For youth in America between the ages of ten and twenty-four, suicide is the third leading cause of death. It results in approximately 4,600 lives lost each year.[20]

Deaths from youth suicide are the greatest tragedy, but it's not the only problem. More young people survive suicide attempts than actually die. They may be emotionally fragile for quite a while. Youth in grades 9–12 from public and private schools throughout the United States were surveyed: When asked about the twelve months preceding the survey, 16 percent reported seriously considering suicide, 13 percent reported creating a plan, and 8 percent reporting trying to take their own life. Each year, approximately 157,000 youth between the ages of ten and twenty-four receive medical care for self-inflicted injuries at emergency departments across the U.S.[21] These are stunning and horrifying statistics.

"In the United States, 70 percent of all deaths among youth and young adults aged 10–24 years result from four causes: motor vehicle crashes (23 percent), other unintentional injuries (18 percent), homicide (15 percent), and suicide (15 percent)."[22]

These numbers illustrate the sad reality of how depression and the desire to escape current circumstances play a part in many teens' realities. Technology can provide an easy first step in escaping.

Rather than let these statistics cripple us with fear, we should let these truths motivate us to help our kids develop healthy coping skills for when life gets hard. Helping kids to find alternatives to screen "scroll potato" behavior—like practicing talking about feelings, asking for help, discussing fears, journaling, looking to the Bible, getting out and taking a walk, and spending time with a friend—will help them avoid suicide and the other "severe" escapes into alcohol, drugs, and cutting.

MOVING AHEAD WITH HOPE

Yes, technology can be a leading reason why a teen might be tired, stressed, overwhelmed, depressed, wanting to escape, or addicted to screens. Yes, there's a perfect storm in our culture that's making life more challenging for this next generation and parenting quite challenging for many who are guiding them. But you and I are not without hope and resources! Technology even brings us many tools and resources for educating ourselves to lead young people toward healthy maturity. Parents can understand the gaps technology overuse can cause in brain and character development and guide their teens toward activities and opportunities to help fill those gaps. Are you ready to jump into discovering your unique role in closing this gap? Let's dig into understanding the power of less and more.

3

LESS AND MORE

I f you have a nagging feeling that technology is negatively influencing your children in one or more ways, you're not alone.
In her *New York Times* article "The Documented Life," Sherry
Turkle says it well: "Technology doesn't just do things for us. It
does things to us, changing not just what we do but who we are."[1]

Perhaps your experiences are similar to blogger Janae Jacobson's. Here's what she writes in a post titled "The iPad Is Stealing
My Son's Childhood":

> I've been observing the behavior of my boys over the last sev-
> eral months. One child is especially drawn to electronics and
> his behavior began to worry me. Although he was only en-
> gaged in technology for 1–2 hours a day (max), he talked
> about video games all the time to anyone who would listen.
> He started sneaking around to play his VTech tablet that he
> got for his birthday and hiding it under his pillow. . . . And

after he played with the iPad or Wii for any length of time, he began to be withdrawn when he was back in the "real world."[2]

Janae's experience illustrates that not every child is sucked into technology but that some children are particularly drawn to it. Janae and her husband began connecting the dots between technology and behavior as they observed changes in one son's actions and personality.

Have you observed your children's behavior changing after they've been playing video games? Are they less patient and more critical and demanding after they've been at the screen for a while? Do they become withdrawn and resistant to engage in conversation with family members because the phone is always in their hands? In their book *Growing Up Social,* Gary Chapman and Arlene Pellicane recommend an easy ABC system to evaluate how technology may be a factor in your child's behavior:

Attitude: What is my child's attitude like after the screen time?
Behavior: How does the content encourage my child to behave?
Character: What character traits are being modeled and picked up?[3]

As you evaluate the effect of screens on your teens, take some specific first steps as a parent. Contrary to what you might think, parent power can be stronger than screen power. Our children are worth the effort it may take to protect them or

Parent power can be stronger than screen power.

win them back from the power of screens. Let's explore some initial steps to take to connect with our kids in this wireless world!

CONNECTING: LESS IS MORE

Model Appropriate Technology Use

After hearing me speak about technology and teens, many parents admit they'll need to change how they use technology if they expect their children to make changes, too. One parent told me, "I've known I needed to do less Facebook and spend more time with my face in a book. This is the motivation I needed."

Parents willing to make changes that benefit their children always encourage me. When our children see we're making adjustments, it's easier for them to change. Also, we increase our empathy for them as they implement our new expectations. Most often, we have to approach technology changes as a family issue rather than just something relevant to our teens.

Randi Zuckerberg, the sister of Facebook founder Mark Zuckerberg, had this to say to parents: "Tech shouldn't replace normal kid activities, but it's not the enemy either. Children will look to their parents to see how it's done. It's important to take some time, whether it's a block on the weekend or an hour every night, to just really unplug and focus on the family."[4]

More Face-to-Face Connecting Zones

To connect more often and more deeply, we can designate places to be technology free. If our children are old enough and mature enough, we can involve them in the decision for more immediate buy-in. Otherwise, "In any given moment, with a buzz or a ping, our devices summon us and we are likely to respond, allowing ourselves to be pulled away from our immediate surroundings and anyone in them, into the waiting world of elsewhere and others."[5]

Our kids need to know that relationships are more than "friending on Facebook," sending quick pics in Snapchat, sharing snippets with the world in Twitter, or whatever social media tool is their favorite to use. A marriage can't be built on texting. A broken heart can't be comforted on Snapchat. A conflict can't be resolved on Twitter. Real relationships require real relationship skills. Determining tech-free connecting zones is one way parents can make sure they are teaching their kids real relationship skills. Let's explore three places you might consider making tech-free zones.

1. Tech-free tables. Eating, including in restaurants, can be designated as family tech-free times. One parent can leave a phone on and have it available, answering it *only* if it's essential. So often in restaurants too many people, including parents, are using handheld devices rather than talking. Even children aged five and younger are playing a game on an iPad or phone. We used to interact with kids to keep them occupied and content, now they take care of themselves. In the past, sometimes older siblings took the initiative to interact and that helped bond sisters and brothers in healthy ways. In our family, my sister-in-law is famous for keeping decks of cards in her purse; her children have played many games of cards in many restaurants over the years.

Recently I saw a stack of six cellphones in the middle of a restaurant table. I introduced myself to the family and told the teens they were fortunate to have parents who wanted to talk with them. The teens agreed! Then one told me if someone reached for a phone before their dad paid the bill, that person had to pay for dinner. We laughed as they admitted that was a strong deterrent.

At home, we can eat as a family without watching television and listening to the radio. Either one can be a reason not to talk to each other. Phones can be off or on silent and placed out of reach. Sharing about our days and planning our tomorrows are much more important than Twitter alerts and Facebook selfies. Connecting through mutually beneficial conversations is essential if we want to influence our kids—and of course, we do.

Find a way to explain your "family times" as blogger Renee Robinson did. She wrote a meaningful letter to her sons explaining her motivation. Her words may inspire you to communicate something similar to your kids as you set tech-free zones.

When we are together, I want all of you. The fullness of you. I want to experience you. Truly experience you. And I can't do that with you when there is an electronic device between us. . . . I want to know you. I want to know your passions. I want to watch you as you discover your God-given talents and gifts. And when you hide behind a screen, I miss out on all of that. And my time with you . . . well it will be over in the blink of any eye. I want to guide you into an understanding of life and who you are. . . . I want to thrive in this life with you. We are in it together. We are a family. . . . When I tell you no to devices, I'm giving you . . . a gift of relationship. True human connection.[6]

After hearing me speak, one mom who made the dinner table a tech-free zone reported that her children now stayed longer at the table and willingly talked with their siblings, her, and her husband. Sometimes their children left their phones on the counter for the rest of the evenings. About one daughter, she reported, "I have heard 'I love you' more in the last two weeks than in a year. She's kind again, sweet, loving, and hanging out with us! Freedom!!"

2. Car conversations and contemplations. The car is another significant place to take back quality time from the mesmerizing power of screens and pods. Talking with each other, simply looking out the window, and daydreaming all serve children well. Sometimes, even though you could run errands more efficiently without your children with you, take them along for the purpose of some focused conversation time.

Rather than popping in a DVD into the player in the car, put on music and sing together or listen to a book on CD and talk about it. When you get in the car, put all of your phones on silent and place them in the glove compartment so you can have conversations without interruptions. You'll be modeling distraction-free driving at the same time. If you get in the car and put your phone on silent and tucked away, your teens will more likely do the same when they start driving.

Kids need quiet and downtime to process and think.

Kids need quiet and downtime to process and think.[7] Especially if you pick them up from school, this mental rest time will be profitable. Because you've been busy all day, you may be tempted to use car time to talk on the phone with a friend or family member. Don't. Prioritize your children instead. They may not ask you to, but they need you to. Use this captured time to talk or encourage them to quiet their minds for a few minutes.

3. Screen-free bedrooms. What's your current policy about your children's bedrooms? Being screen free means they'll better connect with their own thoughts, siblings, and with you when you stop by. Being screen free, especially as bedtime approaches, is especially wise. All people sleep better if they're not looking at screens or playing stimulating games in the hour before their bedtime. Requiring teens to recharge their phones at night in the kitchen is a great habit to start when they first get their phones.

Some parents decide never to permit electronics in their

children's rooms. This means our teens have to use their tools and toys in public parts of our homes. This keeps us more aware of what they're doing on the devices and how much they're using them. Perhaps, if an eReader or iPad is needed to complete homework and your son says he can concentrate better in his room, that's appropriate. Maybe your daughter does well listening to music so you allow her to do that in her room, monitoring occasionally to make sure she's not surfing the Web or playing games.

One family I know keeps a family computer in the kitchen, and they turned their former toy room into a video game room located just off the kitchen. This keeps their major screens out in the open for easy accountability. If the kids borrow Mom's or Dad's laptop they need to use it in family areas of the house. When the kids graduate from high school they get their own laptop and the freedom to use it in their bedrooms. However, all tech products this family owns have Internet filters—even Mom's and Dad's computers. These parents know that it's too easy for parents and kids to end up in the wrong place when using technology. Keeping screens out of bedrooms offers some natural accountability for that and it keeps family members from being isolated from one another.

Transition some parts of your home to a screen-free environment.

Depending on what you currently allow, it may be respectful

to gradually transition some parts of your home to a screen-free environment. Don't expect your kids to be singing your praises if you choose to create screen-free zones. They may balk. They may complain. They may declare they're bored or they have to talk to their friends NOW. They may be angry at first. This is when parenting takes courage. Stand firm and give your kids what they need, not what they want. They will appreciate it someday, but perhaps not until they have kids of their own!

4. No-screen vacations. Vacations are designed to step away from the everyday. However, families with teens often find that teens bring their everyday tech toys with them on vacation. This obstructs family interaction and creates battles during a time that's supposed to be less stressful.

One family had so many battles during a trip to Hawaii, the parents said, "Never again!" They warned their kids, there and then, that all future family vacations would be tech-free. Their teen daughters "argued and attempted negotiations." Vacations for this family have been mostly tech-free ever since. While vacationing, the family uses their phones mostly for GPS, emergencies, and making reservations. The adults sometimes have to check emails periodically because of work-related issues. But the parents stay on their honor not to text, call friends, visit Facebook, or read personal emails while on vacation. At first, the teens dragged their heels but eventually, "they were forced to find other ways to entertain themselves." This family discovered, by removing screens from their vacation time, that one of their daughters, especially, was addicted, "like a drug addict anticipating that next fix." That's been an ongoing struggle for them and their daughter, as there are no quick remedies for long-term addiction. The benefits to the family were generally wonderful. The parents report, "We talked and laughed a lot more. Our kids interacted with us and each other."[8]

FACE-TO-FACE CONNECTING DAYS

About two weeks after recommending parents involve children in choosing one weekend day and one weekday to be screen-free, a ten-year-old boy walked up to me and directly asked, "Are you the lady?" I asked him to elaborate. He asked, "Are you the lady who told my parents we should turn everything off?" Not sure how he'd respond, I think I stepped back a bit before answering, "Yes, I'm Dr. Kathy."

Then I noticed his parents standing against the wall behind him. While confidently maintaining eye contact with me, he responded, "Thank you. I got my daddy back." I audibly gasped. It wasn't at all what I expected to hear. Tears came to my eyes as they met his mom's. She was crying, too.

Though only three digital-free connecting days had passed since the seminar his parents had attended, he and his dad had already been to the park. "I can already throw better!" the boy told me. "And he's teaching me how to play chess. He says I'm smart enough. I think I'll like it. And guess what else? My mom let me help her make cookies because she said we could turn the oven on but just not the plug-in stuff I play with. They were good cookies!"

I'll never forget the dad's heartfelt thanks:

Your challenging idea showed me that my son hadn't left us as much as I had left him. I now put my phone on my dresser when I get home from work. I do this every night, not just Wednesdays. Anybody who really needs us has my wife's number. . . . I used to come home from work and check a website to see what sporting events were on that I'd want to watch. Then I'd check our bank balance and maybe check tomorrow's weather and some news headlines. I realize now that what I intended to take a few minutes was using up valuable time when my children were awake. Now I interact with them before dinner and check the Internet when the kids are in bed.

This isn't an isolated success story. Another parent sent me this note:

We have faithfully kept up with the two media-free days a week. . . . Recently my kids have given a little pushback on the idea. Today at lunch we had a little "meeting" to see what their thoughts were about all of the BOREDOM on media-free days and even on the media days once media was over. . . . we wanted to let them in on the decision making. . . between the three of them, they decided to actually INCREASE to 3 media-free days a week and then the oldest typed up a list of 28 ideas that they brainstormed of what they could do during media free-time. Can't thank you enough for your gentle push in this direction!!

And here's one of my favorite testimonies. Check out all the exclamation marks: "Media-free Sunday!!! They loved it and want to continue!!! Every Sunday media-free!! And we're talking about 3 teenagers!! Thank you, Dr. Kathy!!!"

You will choose to do what works well for you and your family. Identify your frustration points or the screens that seem to get out of hand for your family, and start there. For instance, Janae Jacobson and her husband decided to reserve the iPad and Wii for the weekends only. Their sons are allowed to watch television during the week, but only one minute of television time for every one minute they read. Making these changes in screen time eliminated the majority of negative behaviors after just a few months.[9]

LIVING THROUGH THE LENS

I can remember, long ago, dropping off rolls of film at the store, waiting a week for the pictures to be developed, and then paying for the photos—whether they were good or not. We've come a long way with today's digital cameras and the camera function on our phones and other devices. Most of us carry a camera wherever we go!

Pictures are a beautiful way to stay connected, especially when we don't live close to those we love. I enjoy posting personal and ministry pictures on social media and sharing them with friends and family. I'm glad when they share pictures with me. Pictures often communicate more vibrantly than words. But just because it's easy to take good pictures and post them on social media doesn't mean we always should. Just as with all technology, moderation is appropriate. Let's explore four questions that can guide you to model balance for your kids in social media photo sharing:

We can't afford to be observers looking for the perfect photo op.

Am I Fully Present with My Children?

Often our camera and the photos we want can seem to be a higher priority than our children. To them, it can appear like they're acting in a play and we're the audience. If we want to connect with them, we can't afford to be observers looking for the perfect photo-op. By not really being present with them in the moment, we miss out on joy and opportunities to personally love and influence them.

Leaving our cameras at home sometimes is a good idea, especially when we know we'll be tempted to turn our kids into the subject of too many photos. When we do have it with us, we can make an effort to take more spontaneous photos our kids don't pose for. We can also let them take photos of us and make sure we ask others to take pictures of all of us together.

But rather than looking through your camera screen at your son or daughter, try leaving the phone in your pocket or purse so that you can make eye contact, watch for nuances of facial expression, and soak in the atmosphere of an event. Remind yourself that it's great just to be together.

Should I Share This Moment?

Just because we photograph something doesn't mean we should share it on social media. Some things should remain private and intimate. Children can question whether what we say we just enjoyed was about them or about us sharing them.

A young boy at the playground got all the way across the monkey bars and turned to his mom. He didn't ask, "Did you like it, Mommy?" Rather, he asked, "Did you get a good picture? Was it good enough for Facebook or should I do it again?" What do you want your son to think is important? Him, or a picture or video of him?

My friend Kenny returned from vacation and explained on Facebook that he hadn't taken many pictures of his wife and daughter: "I wanted to soak it all in and not be consumed with capturing every detail. There is a sacredness of just holding some memories to myself."

If you tend to overshare your pictures on social media, sometimes a "media fast" can reestablish your sharing boundaries, bringing them back into moderation. A media fast might be a specific period of time that you'll refrain from sharing pictures on social media.

Is This Picture Good Enough?

Digital photography allows us to easily take numerous photos, trying to get better shots each time. When we don't, we can correct them. We can change lighting, crop out what we don't want, eliminate red-eye, and much more. In her book *No More Perfect Moms*, Jill Savage suggests that this attempt to make things more perfect might be buying into "the perfection infection." Sometimes, in an effort to break the "perfection infection" we should decide the pictures we take are good enough without editing.

We can pay extra to improve children's school pictures. When parents choose to have their children's braces and acne removed, how do the children feel? Unaccepted? Ugly? Rejected? Defective? Could this contribute to feeling pressure to be perfect? To look perfect? Is all this posting on social media causing competition and judgmental comparisons?

After one four-year-old posed for about her eighth picture on the first day of preschool, following her mom's directions to smile more, move out of a tree's shadow, turn more to the right, and the like, she burst into tears. While running away from her mom, she loudly proclaimed, "I thought I was prettier than this!!" Her mom was devastated. Of course she never meant to communicate critique to her daughter; she meant to celebrate that she was growing up. But her daughter took away the message she never intended to send. Being aware of the possibility of sending mixed messages helps us adjust our expectations when it comes to taking snapshots of our kids.

Sometimes it seems we've discarded God's way of seeing us, as if His perspective were irrelevant. First Samuel 16:7 shows us God's priorities: "The Lord does not look at the things people look at. People look at the outward appearance, but the Lord looks at the heart."

> **Extreme narcissists** will usually be isolated and lonely. It's hard for others to be their friends.

Am I Contributing to the Narcissism I Complain About?

Narcissism gets its name from Narkissos, a handsome youth in Greek mythology who fell in love with his own reflection in water after being rejected by a nymph. He pined away, loving only himself. That's the core of narcissism: self-love and being satisfied by contemplating one's self or one's appearance. Extreme narcissists will usually be isolated and lonely. It's hard for others to be their friends.

It's normal for teens to be somewhat self-centered. It's part of their journey to independence. But it's good to evaluate whether your teen is more interested in his or her own appearance, importance, and abilities than you think is healthy and normal. The narcissistic tendencies of this younger generation are definitely on the list of complaints I hear about when I talk with people about today's youth.

But how did today's young people get so focused on themselves? How much of the blame for that belongs to our generation? Could it be that we are unwittingly contributing to the "all-about-me" attitudes so prevalent in this generation? Are you posting a lot of photos from their concerts, sporting events, and parties? Do your social media platforms appear to be more about them than about you? Sometimes our good intentions have unexpected consequences. One friend posted on Facebook about a dance her daughter was going to attend. She commented about the great deal they got on her dress and shoes. How did she end her post? Not with, "I hope she has a great time." No, it ended with, "I can't wait to post pictures!" I'm not sure it crossed her mind what message that might be sending!

Narcissism can result in the regular posting of selfies. Would it surprise you to know that from 2012–2013, the frequency of the use of the word *selfie* increased 17,000 percent? In 2013 Oxford Dictionaries dubbed it the Word of the Year?[10] Teens who are loved well and affirmed honestly at home will be less likely to become preoccupied with selfies.[11]

CONNECTING: MORE IS MORE

Cultivate Quiet

Quiet time promotes better processing and thinking. Periods of quiet also help rejuvenate us when we're overwhelmed and stressed. There's a good reason why God told us to "be still, and know that I am God" (Psalm 46:10). We need quiet in our lives to balance out all the activity.

Many families find ways to build some quiet time into their days. When there are still children in the house young enough for naptime, it's possible to declare quiet hours during the little ones' naptime. Other family members have to go to their rooms or find another quiet corner and play by themselves. To help the youngest ones rest, everyone in the home chooses something quiet to engage in.

With teens, this gets more complicated, but quiet times for them are also valuable. During quiet times, teens discover the value of their innermost thoughts. Quiet helps teens become more comfortable with themselves. They'll know themselves better and discover they don't need to be constantly entertained and distracted. Of course, sitting in front of a screen seems "quiet" because sound is easily muted, or headphones keep the sound personal to a teen. But adding "screen-free" to "quiet" times provides a rest from the constant barrage of images and ideas, allowing a young person's mind to rest.

Quiet helps teens become more comfortable with themselves.

As your teen gets used to quiet times, he or she might need ideas for things to do with that time. This is a great time for personal Bible reading and prayer. Young people can read without the usual backdrop of music. They could try their hand at an old-fashioned thank-you note instead of a text or email. Many teens enjoy journaling or sketching. They might do some stretching exercises. These times of quiet encourage activities that develop parts of the brain not being put to use by their digital pastimes. It's great to provide time and space for teens to slow down, contemplate, and get in tune with themselves and the way God made them.

Read Together

Reading to our children, either one-parent-to-one-teen or together as a family, should never be abandoned just because they hit their teen years! But it gets harder as teens' personal schedules get busier and their homework load gets heavier. Reading together is a powerful connector as you share the enjoyment of the story and build the memory together. Reading to our kids creates an intermission in the middle of life's busyness. It quiets all of us down. Rich emotional bonding can take place during these read-aloud times. Not only that, but reading to teenagers continues to build their listening vocabulary, which improves their reading and learning abilities, one of the best predictors of school success.[12]

Your teens can remember the closeness they felt when you snuggled up on a couch or in bed with a book when they were young. Whether they'll admit it or not, that bonding with you was meaningful. When you read a book, you dive into a new world of events and characters. When you read it *together,* you're sharing those events and relationships! Your teen has a whole world of experiences and relationships apart from you, but your shared reading life is yours *together*. Families develop inside jokes and favorite one-liners from the books they've read together. They have great memories of times when they had to stop the reading because the whole family was laughing so hard—or when they shared the blissful torture of suspense when the reading had to pause at a strategic moment in the storyline. Your teens don't take you along to school or youth group or to hang out with their friends—and that's just how it should be. But diving into reading together provides you with shared adventures and characters. Especially if you have trouble finding enough common ground to have good conversations with your teens, being able to talk about the story you're reading together is a great way to ease into more relaxed communication with them.

If you don't like reading aloud, audiobooks are plentiful these days—and not just for long road trips in the car (though that works really well for helping the family do something together instead of having almost every person in the car isolated by his or her own headphones!).

Today's teens chafe against boredom—and they're easily bored.

So hang on to the pastime of reading together as a family as long as you can. If it seems to have dropped away in the busyness of life, sneak it back in at the holidays or on a road trip. Make some memories as you connect over a great story!

Celebrate Boredom

Today's teens chafe against boredom—and they're easily bored. They run from boredom and attempt to fill every waking moment with something to keep them entertained. But we want them to do more than just accept that boredom is a fact of life. Boredom is better than that! It's actually valuable, so what if we changed the paradigm and taught our teens that it's good to be bored sometimes? We all need to get off the "human-doing treadmill" and rest our minds and bodies.

Times of boredom spark tremendous creativity! It's during the downtimes that teens' brains process and consolidate information.[13] This is good for us busy adults, too. Most of us have had that experience of struggling with a knotty problem—and then suddenly experience the "Aha!" moment while lying down to sleep or when we're in a waiting room somewhere. What I've learned about the benefits of rest, quiet, and boredom reinforce my decision not to listen to music on airplanes and sometimes just sit. I may appear to be doing nothing, but as learning is consolidated and creativity is birthed, new insights regularly leap into my brain!

Boredom cultivates reflection, generates ideas, develops curiosity, increases creativity, and inspires vision. Letting our thoughts wander sparks ideas that might not have been able to surface in the busyness of life. Rather than telling ourselves we're missing out on something important by pushing the pause button on occasion, we need to tell ourselves and our teens that there is much to be gained by allowing boredom to enter our lives every once in a while.

Celebrate Play

When two people play together, strong emotional connections form. This is one reason my brother and I are so close. He and I always played together, and we still do! My brother and his three children, now young adults, are close and enjoy each other so much because they have always played together and still do.

In their book *The Big Disconnect*, Catherine Steiner-Adair and Teresa Barker talk about the power of play:

It is this "just being together"—really together—with parents and family that gives children confidence, pride, and security. They feel they belong, they feel the connection, and they are more likely to talk about things that matter to them in that setting than at any other time. . . . In addition to family play, a child's solo and peer play nurtures curiosity, grit, and zest and a host of social and emotional learning closely linked to well-being and success in school and life. Play is where children discover their own talents and inspiration. It is where they practice concentration and how to work through frustration. Play is the best fertilizer for growing kids.[14]

Sometimes a parent's style of play can take the teens by surprise. They're just not expecting Dad to sneak up, ninja-style, with a can of Silly String or Mom suddenly to whip out a deck of cards and shuffle and deal like a cardsharp! Drag out the board games on a rainy night. For sure, make the most of power outages (hide the batteries if you have to!) for playing games or telling stories.

One friend of mine found that when she and her husband invented seasonal games, her children immediately made those into family traditions—and looked for them to happen again the next year. They hide their kids' Easter baskets along with the eggs and make them hunt for them (they do it on the Saturday of Holy Week to keep it off the celebration of Resurrection Sunday). They have a treasure hunt late on Christmas Day, hours after the regular presents have been opened and enjoyed. The clues are goofy and take the kids all over the house. The treasure box usually holds books or art supplies, wrapped for Christmas. When the kids were little and they made caramel apples for the first time, she and her husband kidnapped the plate of apples while they were cooling and left a trail of clues for the kids. Now they expect caramel apples to disap-

Thinking leads to thanking.

pear *every* time the family has them. Her kids are high school and college students now, and guess what? They haven't yet outgrown their joy in the family "games."

There's a timeworn saying that the "family who prays to-gether stays together." I'd add, "the family that plays together stays together" too. When your teens see that you enjoy being with them, those deep core needs for security and belonging and identity are being fed.

Cultivate Gratefulness

Grateful children act less entitled and are more content. They're less selfish, self-centered, argumentative, and demanding. We'll dig into these character issues in the next chapters as we discover how technology and gratitude are related. For now, let's simply understand the importance of growing grateful kids.

Thankfulness is actually an old Anglo-Saxon word that means "thinkfulness."[15] Thinking leads to thanking. I'm not talking about teens who say "thank you" because their dads glare at them. I'm talking about *grateful* being who we are, not just what we do and say. Gratitude can be a built-in part of our identities. This is what allows us to be thankful "in all circumstances" (1 Thessalonians 5:18).

The first and best way your kids will grow in thankfulness is for you to practice being thankful—and verbalizing your feelings of gratitude, toward God and toward others. If this kind of speaking up about your feelings of thankfulness feels awkward, start small, maybe by expanding your thanks as you pray over meals or by speaking up about one thing you feel thankful for, perhaps when you're driving your teen somewhere. As you speak your thankfulness, it will become easier and more natural for you.

If your teens need to wake up to how much they really have, it can jumpstart their thankfulness to get them out and about with people who have significant needs. Any local food pantry would joyfully welcome teen volunteers (or family volunteers)! Many youth groups offer teens opportunities to serve the under-resourced or the homeless, especially at the holidays or in the cold winter months. Many elementary schools have mentoring or tutoring programs for their at-risk students and would be glad for teen helpers. If your teens have the chance to travel to emerging countries, that can be an eye-opener for them as well. Your teens may be aware of world and poverty issues via their screens, but seeing images doesn't carry the immediacy of real-life interaction with people who are needier than they are. Help create opportunities for your children to find their gratitude!

LESS AND MORE!

We've explored teens' core needs and their unique traits, and now we've established some basic less-and-more guidelines. We need to modify some of the practices that have crept into our lifestyle. Some things definitely need to be *less*—less screen time and noise to overwhelm, stress, and fatigue our teens. And there are some things we want to do *more*—more family connection, more books, more quiet, more play, more boredom, more gratitude.

We can turn our attention to the specific lies that come through—overtly or covertly—to our teens through the technology in their lives. We have the privilege and responsibility to help debunk these false messages and to introduce truth to change the minds of the young people we love.

4

LIE #1: I AM THE CENTER OF MY OWN UNIVERSE

For as long as I can remember, I've been a bit of a clean freak about my glasses. I keep a hot-pink cloth for cleaning them in my purse. I have a white one by the chair in my den, a gray one in an office desk drawer, and a blue one in a bathroom drawer. It totally bugs me when my glasses aren't clean. Any fingerprint smudge can make what I'm looking at appear out of focus.

Having the right prescription is more important. The slightest improvement can make a huge difference with corrective lenses. Many times, I thought I was seeing just fine until my annual checkup. A minor adjustment felt major; I hadn't realized how out of focus things had become.

You've got an invisible pair of glasses—and so does your teen. Those are the lenses through which you look at life. If the glasses are out of focus with the wrong prescription, we won't see things accurately. Right things can look wrong, and wrong things can look right.

These metaphorical glasses are our basic worldview.[1] Our particular prescription is made up of our beliefs and assumptions that act as our filter. We interpret what we see, hear, think, feel, and experience through our prescription. Therefore, what we believe and assume will influence everything new. What we think we "clearly" know may be a bit blurry without us realizing it. We react to everything based on the beliefs that make up our prescription.

For example, you could enter a contest and win the newest and greatest tablet. Your worldview—your prescription—determines how you interpret your victory. If you believe in fate, you may think, *It's my lucky day!* If you believe you're the most important person in the universe and the world revolves around you, you may think, *I don't know why everyone is so surprised or upset. It makes total sense I'd win because I deserve to win.* If you believe Jesus is Lord over everything, you may think, *I sure don't deserve this good gift, but I thank You for it, Lord. Show me how to be a good steward of Your generosity.*[2]

Without realizing it, teens have become their own gods.

Based on observations and study, we can say this generation's prescription of beliefs and assumptions are frequently *not* centered in the God of the Bible or a relationship with Jesus Christ. This is often the case even for those who claim to know and love Him. Rather, their worldview is centered in themselves. They and their technology are most important. Without realizing it, they've become their own gods.

Many young people make decisions only with themselves in mind. This has been true of many teens throughout time, but this kind of self-on-the-throne does seem to be at an all-time high. Teens can behave as if the world revolves around them—or at least as if they wish it did! My coworker, project manager Nancy Matheis, visualizes their worldview as a wheel. Each teen is at the center of his or her world. The spokes, representing things like family, peers, ideas, goals, school, church, media, and other technology, all point to them. All these aspects of their lives are in place and designed to serve them.

A Christian worldview could also be represented by a wheel. God would be at the center of that wheel, the hub where all the spokes meet. The spokes He created and influences would go out from His heart. Each of us represents one of many, many spokes. He designed us to serve and glorify Him. Therefore, spokes representing believers radiate outward but also point back to God.

When talking about how intertwined teens have become with their technology, Randy Thomas, our online content and social media manager, offered this wise word:

> Being connected meets a core spiritual need to connect with a force greater than themselves and they believe the Internet is the fount of all truth. Searching the Internet for personal answers, direction, and worth has increasingly supplanted seeking

God's input through prayer. The high priests are the technology, which facilitates transactions with a power greater than themselves. They don't get ideas from acknowledged leaders or chief proponents who represented those ideas, as people would have done in Bible times or many of us did in our youth. Rather, they're being led by and taught by their technology to believe that a way to transcend the everyday machinations of life is to simply login.

Clearly, a main reason to know our teens' worldview is that it heavily influences what they understand about God and how they'll relate to Him. And we desperately need to understand our own worldview because our prescription influences how we parent our children and who we hope they will become. They're watching us and listening. We must take our role modeling seriously.

Many of our young people are wearing glasses with the prescription "It's all about me" or "I am the center of my own universe." Many of our teens may understand God as someone who meets their needs and keeps them happy. They don't wonder about humanity's relationship to God because it's God's relationship with them *personally* that matters. God serves them; they don't serve God. The idea that God is His own Person, with His own ideas that won't always agree with theirs, is a completely foreign thought. They are blinded enough by the glare of their screens to not be able to see through His prescription. (Notice that I use the phrase *many of our teens.* I'm very grateful for every Christian teen who knows, loves, serves, and glorifies God with his or her worldview!)

As I ponder and pray for this generation particularly and for all of us as well, Marshall McLuhan's words from his 1964 book *Understanding Media* come to mind: "Societies have been shaped more by the nature of the media men use to communicate than by the content of the communication."[3] More than fifty years later, his words are still ringing true.

The I-am-the-center-of-my-own-universe lie is so influential and controlling that I call it an "umbrella worldview lie." Teens believe the other lies partly because they first think they are the center of their own universe.

Let's examine this lie further and explore the reasons teens believe the lie, how it influences their beliefs and behaviors, and what we can do about it. As we explore this lie and the ones in the chapters just ahead, keep applying what you read to your personal situation with your particular children. Your particular children will have their own strengths and weaknesses that may make them more susceptible to the influence of certain lies. You know your children best! As you begin to understand the lies driving some of your children's beliefs and behaviors and read about possible methods for replacing lies with the truth, you will gravitate toward some suggestions more than others. You will also develop your own solutions—the best ones for your own family.

God's Word, with its rich instruction, will also shape our

understanding of these lies and and lead us toward what is true. It will be our guide as we help our teens trade lies for the truth.

EVIDENCE OF THE LIE:
REASONS WHY AND THINGS TO TRY

My Parents Make Me the Center

Parents sometimes over-prioritize their children. Children should know they're important to their parents. But, as we teach at Celebrate Kids, anything well done, overdone, is badly done. Too much attention reinforces the prescription "It's all about me."

As Jill Savage and I point out in our book *No More Perfect Kids*, when we hover over our children, constantly making sure they're okay and attending what they're doing, we communicate, "I can't live without you."[4] As a result, kids can develop an inflated and unhealthy view of themselves.

The number of pictures, videos, and status updates some parents post of their children on Facebook and other social media contributes to children believing they make the world go 'round. I'm not opposed to us posting pictures or updates about our children. But this shouldn't be *all* we post. If it is, our teens can feel we're meeting *our* needs for security, identity, and belonging in them. They may believe their purpose is to keep us happy and they're only competent when they do. More than one teen has proclaimed to me, "I wish my mom would get a life!" (Occasionally they'll say "parents," but I usually hear this complaint about moms.)

Children who believe they are the center of the universe can come to feel that they're entitled. They think they deserve people's attention and may act out to get it. (Does anyone in Hollywood come to mind?) When their worldview is "The world revolves around me," it's easy for them to become self-absorbed and demanding. They may even treat others with disdain and contempt. They'll be selfish in their friendships and prideful about accomplishments. Even things done well with others will be centered around them to keep this lie in place. As you can imagine, all of this self-focus negatively affects relationships. Teens may actually be lonely, and they won't experience the joy of loving others sacrificially or helping others generously.[5]

So what can you do to compensate for this over-prioritizing your children, if you identify that this has been happening in your family? Many positive steps will help reverse this negative pattern!

God created the world to display Himself. The world is about Him and for Him.

1. We can apologize. If we recognize our kids are behaving as if they're more important than others and we may be partly responsible because of how we prioritize them, we can apologize. We can discuss what beliefs and choices caused this and determine how to relate instead.

2. We can introduce them to Jesus. Knowing Jesus as their personal Savior and Lord helps them understand the world doesn't revolve around them. When they know they're following

Jesus, they're less likely to expect people to follow them.

3. We can teach them about creation. Let's teach that God created the world to display Himself. The world is about Him and for Him.[6] Understanding this moves God to the rightful place in their world.

4. We can help them understand why God created them. Starting as soon as possible (when kids are young—or right now!), it's important to communicate that each of us is important because God created us and He didn't have to. He wanted to! Each teen is created in His image (Genesis 1:27) and for His glory (Isaiah 43:7). We're created uniquely (Psalm 139:14) the way He wanted us to be (Ephesians 2:10). When we act as if we we're created for our own glory or we see our kids doing the same, we must stop and do some self-reflection in light of these verses. Then we can change our behaviors to reflect God's will and not our own whims.

5. We can provide volunteer opportunities. One of the surest ways to show teens they don't make the world go 'round is to help them get their eyes off themselves by helping others. Doing something together is especially effective because you can affirm your teen's strengths and attitudes as you work side by side. You can then talk about how it felt to put others first. Understanding *how* your teens are smart can help discover activities they'll be good at and enjoy. There are many kinds of intelligence strengths, and identifying your teens' particular gifts can direct them to specific service ministries. Celebrate Kids offers resources to help you discover types of intelligence.[7]

Technology Can Be about Only What We Like and Want

The use of technology can cause any of us to become self-centered. It's so focused on the consumer! If you trawl online one afternoon for a certain kind of T-shirt or new boots, advertisers for T-shirts and boots will appear on your Facebook news feed for weeks. When you buy a book on Amazon.com or borrow one via a library app, book suggestions will appear, tailored just for you based on your buying preferences and books that other people bought who also purchased the book you did. That computer seems to know you and be conforming to your particular needs! The computer reinforces the untruth: It's all about me!

But believing what the computer seems to be telling us can lead us straight toward ignoring people around us and their expectations of us. We're so used to having things our own way, we can become inordinately demanding, always wanting what we want. Without intervention, impressionable teens with their brains still developing are at greater risk of negative beliefs and behaviors becoming the norm than those of us who are older.

Teens can scroll social media, paying attention to who likes their posts. They can comment on what they want to. They may ignore those who ignore them. When they do comment on other posts, it's often with the intent of drawing attention to themselves. They are in control of what they like, where they spend their moments online, and who or what they'll ignore or pay attention to.

Using search engines and certain websites, teens can investigate what they want to. They can ignore what they decide is irrelevant. They may be curious about a celebrity in their current favorite movie. They may look up details about the launch of a new game. School assignments will engage them for at least a while, but if they decide they're irrelevant it will be challenging for them to put forth much effort. Teachers tell me about their students' constant complaints, quick boredom, and how quickly they disengage. This lie that they are the center of their own universe and the priority that everything must be personally relevant are among the causes of high school and college dropout rates being as high as they are. Sometimes students are apathetic because they expect their teachers to serve them and their specific interests and desires; they've lost the ability to realize that their teachers have a whole classroom of other students to tend and that they must step up to the plate and take initiative to create forward momentum academically.

Teens can listen to music they like by creating their own radio "stations" at sites like Pandora and Spotify. Rather than purchasing a whole album, they can buy just the songs they want at iTunes. They can download a song they hear and like with an app on their phone. With buds in their ears, they can listen to what they want when they want, as many times as they want, and tune out whatever else is going on and what doesn't immediately interest them personally.

Similarly, many teens can watch what they want, when they want, on whatever device they want to use. Times have changed a lot since the days when a family had one screen in the home—

usually a television with three or four stations. If a teen's parents were home, the teen didn't even have control over what the family would watch. With cable offering dozens of stations and immediate streaming easily downloadable to any computer or smartphone, family members can watch in any and every room in the house!

Movies on Demand, streaming options, the DVR, Redbox, DVDs we own, and pausing live TV—all of these options give power and choice to the individual consumer and thus support the lie that the world revolves around me. It's easy to see how these services, as wonderful as they are, contribute to self-centeredness and isolation. We're together in the same home, but not connected or connecting to each other. We can watch things downloaded onto devices while in public and never need to talk to anyone. The constant availability of shows and movies we want to watch allows us to avoid anything that doesn't keep us happy. In other words, relational time and opportunities are being usurped by personal media consumption.

Relational time and opportunities are being usurped by personal media consumption.

So how can parents counteract the influence of this media-option overload and the way it can reinforce teens' misperception that they are the center of the universe? We can move media use into community and away from individual emphasis in many positive ways.

1. We can share music, television shows, movies, and games. Let's get to know what our teens like and why they like it and invite them to interact with us and the media resources we like. We can make the effort to listen and watch together and discuss the experience.

2. We can help them widen their media choices by growing their interest in specific problems or issues. We can ask them about the problems they may be interested in solving so we can help them see the relevance of content being taught at church and school. To expand their interests, we can introduce them to local mentors who are doing important work, peruse relevant websites with them, and watch related videos online. We can remind them during teachable moments that we're each alive to leave the world a better place by using our gifts and talents, which brings good pleasure to the One who created us.

3. We can help them take initiative in their academics. As teens get older, they need to get ready for real-life workplaces or for real-world, post-high school academic experiences. Their days of having teachers "hold their hands" are soon going to be a memory! Unlike the world of technology, which tailors itself to accommodate and please each consumer, adult life has a way of expecting proactive decision-making and initiative. So rather than have teachers or parents closely monitor their homework schedules, teens should be encouraged to take the lead in organizing their time and tasks for academic success. Teens should begin to take responsibility for making their academic and work dreams come to fruition.

One family asked me to meet with their college son who was in danger of not graduating because of his academic apathy. He was having a hard time making the jump from having his teachers and professors spoonfeed him with projects and assignments to finding direction for his own future. In this case, technology played both a negative and a positive role. Technology had damaged his initiative by reinforcing his "entitled" feeling that everything should be orchestrated toward him and for him, making life easy. At the same time, technology had connected this young man with the larger world and its problems. When I asked him what he saw in the world that he would like to fix, he lit up and talked nonstop. He became animated and enthused about his future. I suggested he relate course content and assignments to these problems and solutions when possible. I explained that this was his job and not his professors'. This was not something he'd ever considered. He found great motivation and ended up having a successful senior year.

4. We can really know our kids. When we know our kids and affirm their unique giftedness, they have less need to define their uniqueness by their screen-time choices. I recently asked a high school senior what she definitely wanted her teachers to know about her. She answered, "I'm an individual. I'm not like everyone else." As Jill Savage and I included in *No More Perfect Kids*, children need to be treated as unique individuals.[8] It's one of the ways they know they're known. It establishes an appropriate understanding of their value so they won't need everyone paying attention to them for superficial reasons. We must get to know our kids. They may act like they don't care and they may resist our attempts to ask about their day and their lives. We can't give up. Be present, observant, and politely persistent. Our teens need us to help them grow and develop their unique identity.

Who I Connect with Is My Decision!

Just as we can decide what to listen to and watch, technology gives us the freedom to decide who to talk with, befriend, and ignore. Staying in control of this is one of the ways young people stay the center of their own universe.

Teens can't control who shows up at a party or who knocks on their dorm-room door, but they can control who they talk with by phone, text, Skype, and who they interact with on social media. This power and control makes them feel important and comfortable.

There's nothing wrong with communicating online or having important digital relationships. Many of my own friendships have been strengthened by the ease of texting, emailing, and connecting on sites like Facebook. This is true for longtime friends and family I was connected with long before these methods were available. It's also true for new relationships that started online. Of course, we know just a slice of someone's life when communicating only online and that can never replace offline interaction.

While I'm writing this chapter, a friend's daughter, April, is in South Africa on a mission trip. April and her mom have been able to text each other. It's important to April's parents to know she is okay. But more than basic "proof of life," they love hearing about her experiences, and April clearly enjoys sharing with them. Technology is allowing them to stay connected. Of course, if April didn't share regularly about her normal, everyday experiences in college, she wouldn't be texting from Africa.

> **We need to** make sure we don't equate online interactions as having the same value as offline relationships.

Remember, for teens, it's all about the relationship. April knows her parents care, and she wants to connect with them every way possible.

Relationship issues get more complicated when teens relate to others only or mostly online. This may stunt teens' social skills and increase loneliness even though they have many "friends" on their social networks. A conversation a number of years ago with a teenager motivated my study of this topic. He admitted to having "no real friends." He had friends he gamed with, but he admitted no one really knew him and he didn't know them either. His loneliness frustrated and isolated him.

Teens need to stay connected to people they choose to communicate with. That's why keeping their phone on and with them is important. If they're on social media sites, having access to them matters. They need to be able to comment on posts important to them and update people on what they're doing. Yet, at the same time, being constantly connected can increase their stress: "The steady pattern of reassuring texts can also become a drumbeat of obligation many teens find exhausting."[9] It's a bit of a catch-22. They're stressed if they're connected. They're stressed if they're not. Many young people admit it's hard for them to take a break.

When their phone rings, they'll pay attention to the ring tone or look to see who's calling or texting. They'll rarely answer if the number isn't already in their phone. They will answer if they're in the mood to talk with that person, even if they're in the middle of another conversation. Although those of us who are older may think it's rude when they ignore us, they think it's rude to ignore who's on the phone. They can't risk angering that person or missing out on something happening online.

Communicating is a strength of our wireless world. However, there's no guarantee this communication will lead to connection. That's the challenge for all of us. It's an even larger issue for young people who have learned to develop online and offline relationships at the same time. We all need to pay attention to make sure we don't equate online interactions as having the same value as offline relationships.

Authenticity, vulnerability, and accountability may not come naturally, even within our own families. We must not give up nor can we afford to be distracted by our own technology. Each of us has a core need to belong. Therefore, being connected but not really connecting with others creates deep stress and leaves a gap in our hearts.

So how can we help our kids relax their tight control over their relationship universe?

1. We can teach friendship skills. Modeling, talking about, and directly instructing our kids about friendship skills is wise. As Chapman and Pellicane point out in *Growing Up Social,* "The next generation is at great risk of losing the art of personal conversation. But you can intentionally teach your children to get along and to value others face to face."[10] I absolutely agree! We have to help our kids develop friendship skills, including self-evaluation, communication, choosing friends, maintaining friendships, resolving conflicts, and ending relationships. For example, to help with choosing friends and deciding whether to end a friendship, we can teach the difference between consistent character flaws and an occasional mistake in judgment.[11]

2. We can help our kids identify friendship levels. Not every casual relationship should become a friendship. Our kids need to learn who to trust—and who not to trust. Not everyone can be trusted with our intimate feelings and thoughts.[12]

3. We can help our kids learn to read body language. Because our teens have less experience with offline conversations, helping them learn to interpret facial expressions and body language will increase their confidence and improve their social skills. They then may be willing to engage in more face-to-face interactions. These are part of a people-smart skill set.[13]

4. We can recognize that technology sometimes offers a "safety net" for teens' communication with parents. Teens sometimes use their tech tools even with parents because they feel safest when doing so. I heard of one teen who used email to connect with his mom so that he could say to her what was too hard for him to say to her in person: Please stop drinking. His mom read the email and privately thought about what he was asking of her. By the end of that day, this woman entered a rehabilitation program—and she continues to do well.

5. We can model and teach "one-anothering." The New Testament offers many instructions to love, serve, encourage, admonish, and build up one another. These verses can help teens understand that connecting with others is a privilege and an opportunity to bless others and better themselves. Their mood and whether they already know people should not be their primary filter when deciding which people to talk with. These truths— which include living in peace with one another, honoring one another, being devoted to one another, and not judging one another—could be the focus of family devotions or brought up at teachable moments.[14]

6. We can teach them how to introduce themselves. When working with groups of teens, plan time for them to get to know each other. It won't be easy for them to do it on their own. Jonathan, a high school student, aptly represents how many teens feel: "We don't even introduce ourselves. Teachers just say, 'Okay, you're in physics.' Everybody's looking around thinking, *That person's cooler than me, that person's not as cool as me, that person's hair doesn't look good today.* When I become a teacher, the first thing

I'll do is take however long it takes until people get comfortable."[15] I think Jonathan is on to something healthy!

God is the center of the wheel, and we are the spokes.

THE TRUTH WE WANT TEENS TO BELIEVE

What's the truth we want our kids to believe instead of this lie that they are the center of their own universe? It goes back to the spoke-and-wheel analogy: God is the center of the wheel, and we are the spokes. The truth is: *God is the center of the universe. I'm important, but no more important than anyone else. Relating in healthy ways online and offline will help me believe this.*

We can help dislodge the lie in our teens' hearts and replace it with truth. That truth will move the focus off of them and onto God. It will root out self-centeredness and replace it with a servant heart that cares for others. This truth will serve them well not only as teens but throughout their lifetime as contributing citizens of this world.

Lie #1: I am the center of my own universe.
Truth #1: God is the center of the universe.

Seek the Kingdom of God above all else, and live righteously, and he will give you everything you need.

MATTHEW 6:33 NLT

101

5

LIE #2: I DESERVE TO BE HAPPY ALL THE TIME

It's very likely that no child has ever looked you in the eye and proclaimed, "I deserve to be happy all the time!" They haven't texted you those exact words either. No, they don't say these words. They may not realize they even believe this lie, yet their behavior indicates it's influencing them.

I'm not against happiness. If I'm forced to choose between happiness or misery, I'd choose happiness every time. So would you, and so would the teens we love. But we can't always make happiness happen. It's not a guarantee or something we deserve. Teens who assume constant happiness is possible have unrealistic expectations of this world and will often find themselves frustrated.

Happy everything. Every time. Everywhere. Everyone. This pop-culture mantra is prevalent and controlling. But here's the reality: We can't be happy all the time. We can, however, experience an internal joy that is not dependent on our circumstances. This is the truth that refutes the happiness lie. This is where we want to lead our teens.

Perhaps the first thing to do is to humbly ask ourselves if and how we've contributed to our teens' expectation of personal happiness. For example, do we give in at times rather than standing our ground because we, too, want to be happy all the time? Are we avoiding their disappointment, anger, conflict, and the ensuing argument even though we know saying no would be better for them? Of course parents are delighted when their children are truly happy. Yet when it is more important to correct or answer no, can we not handle a few minutes of personal discomfort for a greater cause?

Whether we were parented well or not can make a difference. If we saw our parents "be the parent" and not cave in to our whining, arguing, or begging, we may have a firmer backbone when it comes to standing firm against the demands of children. Sometimes age can make a difference, too. Young parents who also use lots of technology (and may have bought into this lie themselves) may struggle the most with wanting to keep their kids happy. Our own busyness can make a difference. When we're tired, frustrated, and overwhelmed, we might be tempted to let our teens play another game or text with a friend during dinner. We may buy them another movie. We want to keep them happy and out of our way because we too are pursuing our own happiness.

However, being a parent means it's not about us; it's about

them. It's not just about happiness that happens today; it's about training and learning that lasts a lifetime. It's not about simply being satisfied today; it's about being content today and tomorrow. It's not about temporary peace; it's about permanent joy. We need to parent them well so they'll know these differences. We need to be willing to make tough decisions and experience children's temporary wrath when necessary. It's not about our children being happy all the time. It's about us doing our job as parents.

Teens need parents—and you are their parent, more than and before you are their friend. As you evaluate your role in this lie, don't be afraid to admit where you've believed the lie of happiness yourself and even contributed to their belief of the lie. Teens can respect a "parenting do-over" if you respect them enough to share what you're learning. If you decide changes in the way you relate to your teen are in order, talk with your teen so he or she is not blindsided. Otherwise it might appear that you've become mean all of a sudden, resulting in even more resistance from your teen. You want teens to understand that you will be reestablishing your leadership position in their lives. They haven't become "bad" overnight, but you've determined to do what's right and best for the long term. In time they will get on board, and in the long run they'll respect you for taking your parenting role seriously.

Let's look more deeply at this lie that happiness is deserved. Let's explore the reasons teens believe the lie, what fuels their beliefs and behaviors, and what we can do to replace this lie with a truth that will serve them well.

EVIDENCE OF THE LIE:
REASONS WHY AND THINGS TO TRY

We Live in a Culture of Now

We are experiencing the culture of now. Our teens think they can have what they want when they want it. Now. They have good reason because nowadays everything seems always to be available. Google. Siri. GPS. iTunes. Redbox. Netflix. Movies on Demand. DVR. Digital pictures. Facebook. Apps.

I remember when online shopping wasn't available and shopping took time and effort. I remember the days before online streaming when videos had to be rented from a store; that meant I had to drive there, park, go in, search, choose something, wait in line, pay for it, drive home, watch it, and return it soon after. I can remember looking up numbers and addresses in actual, paper phone books—and unfolding paper maps to figure out how to get from here to there. The business of living took a lot of horsing around; it definitely wasn't the culture of now.

Many teens have FOMO— the fear of missing out.

When today's teens don't get what they want the way they want it right now, many complain and argue. They may accuse us of not caring for them. Subconsciously they may think our job is to keep them happy. Each of us, on the way to adulthood, developed some narcissistic tendencies. It's considered a normal part of development.

However, this generation has taken it to the extreme and the self-focus is lasting much longer.

The culture of now is a cause of self-centeredness. Smart phones have definitely contributed to this. Teens hate turning theirs off or to "silent" for even a short time. Many have FOMO—the fear of missing out. They want to know what's going on as it's happening. Now.

Let's be honest: Some parents have FOMO, too. We have grown accustomed to knowing what's going on in our friends' lives through Facebook. We are used to real-time news and knowing what's going on in the world. We're afraid if we don't log in we'll miss out on something we need to know.

So what can we do to battle this culture of now—in our lives and in the lives of our teens? We can take some steps in the right direction. There's hope for us and the next generation to learn that happiness is circumstantial but joy is eternal.

1. We can implement screen-free days and occasions. To combat self-centeredness that sometimes displays as a fear of missing out, we can institute days and places free from digital distractions. This forces us and our kids to truly interact. Our teens need to discover they can live without knowing constantly what's going on with their friends. When the world doesn't end and relationships don't fail when they've been disconnected for a few hours, they realize they may have more freedom than they thought. No one's happiness should be determined by how often they comment on posts or how quickly people text them back.

2. We can mentally note and carefully call attention to what happens during tech-free times. During planned tech-free times, make mental notes of how long it takes your children to calm down, focus, and engage with the family. See if you can find times when they are obviously enjoying themselves and forgetting their phones. Tactfully, without inordinate attention, encourage them to discover they're happy without being tied to some screen or smart phone.

3. We can present them with opportunities to help and serve others. Nothing gets the focus off self better than directing focus on others! Getting out among people, especially with the goal of meeting others' needs, will wake teens up to activities and events and people they may be missing. They will be reminded of the human side of this world and the needs around them. Whether it's helping an elderly neighbor with yard work or serving a meal at the homeless shelter, our teens need to get a new perspective of what's happening "now."

We Live in a Culture of Impatience

The culture of impatience is very real. The "now culture" addressed above can cause impatience. So can speed. So much is quick today—texting, social media updates, email, research through search engines, apps, one-click-of-the-mouse writing and editing, developing pictures, and scoring on games. High-speed is our new norm and what we're used to. Our teens have never experienced life without high-speed response; it has always been their normal.

Their brains are so used to information coming at them quickly that they're easily distracted when there's a speed or information deficit. When we talk too slowly, the video loads too slowly, the action in a movie moves too slowly, or even Grandma moves too slowly down the hall, teens can find focus challenging. This can cause young people to appear to have ADHD, even when they don't.

When specifically addressing how impatience affects learning and school, my mentor about this generation, author Scott Degraffenreid, put it this way in his book *Understanding the Millennial Mind*: "They're actually just thinking a lot faster. It is not attention deficit, so much as information deficit. They have already thought about what you have shown them and moved on and are waiting for you to show them something else."[1] Scott refers to teens as "learning machines that operate at fire hose volume and wither and disengage when offered the eyedropper quantities of information available in a traditional classroom."[2] I'm humbled when I realize the amount of information young people are able to process and think about.

Is waiting a dying art? Is self-control even a recognizable virtue? What attitudes show up when you and your kids must wait at a doctor's office, for something to arrive in the mail, or for a class to begin? When something is slow, how long does it take before we complain? Are long lines at drive-through restaurants frustrating because of all the complaints you have to listen to from the back seat? When teens are stopped at a red light, can they just sit and wait for the light to change to green, or do they always grab their phones? Do teens yell at their computers when they're slow? Do they complain when having to wait for dinner? Do we?

After a convention, one mom told me about a conversation she overheard when she was out for ice cream with her family. Some young teen girls were talking when one of them said, "It bothers me to brush my teeth. I'm serious! It bothers me. I mean, it takes an ENTIRE two minutes. I wish someone would just invent a swish that cleaned and flossed and just did everything." This mom said she sat there, stunned, thinking, "Did she really just say that?"

Waiting is a part of life.

So we're an increasingly impatient culture! Knowing that, we can take steps—though they may feel counterintuitive at first—to improve our waiting skills and move our teens toward patience.

1. We can pay attention to how we handle waiting. Notice how long it takes before you become impatient. What do you (and your teens) observe in you when you are? Resist the urge to complain. Instead make simple, calm statements like, "Waiting is a part of life," or "We're so used to instant everything. There are still things in the world that take time and require us to wait—and that's okay."

2. We can talk about patience and self-control as fruits of the Spirit. When talking with church youth groups about this topic, I tell them, "God will not rewrite the Bible for your generation. Patience will always and forever be a fruit of the Spirit."[3] Sometimes I challenge those who know Christ: "Are you following Christ, or aren't you? Do you claim God is your everything and that 'I can do all things through him who strengthens me'?[4] Does 'all things' include everything except being patient?" You'd think teens would find my words too in-your-face, but they always receive it well. Today's teens are ready to be challenged to be who they can be.

3. We can talk with our kids about "patience." We can look for examples in our everyday lives of patient people and how they made a difference. We can talk about inventors, musicians, explorers, Bible heroes, and others who were patient and how it mattered. (Walt Disney, for example, was fired by a newspaper editor because he had no good ideas! He went bankrupt several times before he built Disneyland.[5] That's some patience!) We might undertake a word study of "patience," searching for it throughout Scripture. Look for teachable moments to talk about times we didn't wait and how we wish we would have. We can also talk about how to wait and why.

4. We can talk about respect and its role in our patience. Our attitudes toward people influence whether we'll be patient or not. If our kids think we're their servants and it's our job to meet their needs, solve their problems, and keep them happy, they won't be patient. Talk about respect in the family and outside of the family.

5. We can work to eliminate the double standard. Kids find it confusing if we tell them dinner is ready or we're ready to leave for church or the park, and they come when called but then have to wait because we weren't ready. All of us must work on being people who are trustworthy and whose word is true. Patterns may be set, but they can be changed. Let's honor our children, raise our expectations, affirm them when they're patient for even a few minutes, and do the same for ourselves so we improve.

6. We can talk about waiting on God. Learning to wait has huge implications for our kids' emotional and spiritual maturity. They must learn to wait for God's leading and answers when they pray. We know, from several Scriptures, that God wants us to wait hopefully and expectantly.[6] Do we model this for our kids? Our behavior puts our beliefs on display. Waiting on God might be one of the most important things to do in our quick-paced, I-want-it-my-way culture.

> **Avoiding discomfort** can result in underdeveloped personal security, limited identity, and spiritual immaturity.

We Live in the Culture of Easy

We are experiencing the culture of easy. This most certainly causes teens to think happiness is always possible and readily attainable. We can have music and phones with us at all times. We can auto-correct, filter, and crop pictures. Our DVR makes it simple to record television shows to watch at our convenience. Writing is made easier because of functions like copy-and-paste and grammar checks on the computer. These and other tools can eventually help teens improve their writing. They're not bad tools, we just don't want teens to assume everything should be easy because of them.

Teens tend to avoid things they can't do well in order to stay happy. Correcting mistakes, persevering, and asking for help makes them uncomfortable and insecure. They want things to be easy, and they cut-and-run or x-out when they're not. They're used to the identity of "I can do it myself."

Avoiding real or perceived pain keeps them happy, and this concerns me. It's suffering that leads to perseverance, character, and hope (Romans 5:1–5). Avoiding discomfort can result in underdeveloped personal security, limited identity, and spiritual immaturity. It also contributes to not knowing how to work hard. One college teacher told me how she had assigned some research over the weekend. Within twenty-four hours of her Friday class time, three students had emailed her and indicated that they couldn't do the research because she hadn't given them the links to use. She had to tell them that she expected them to find their own resources, do their own research, and make their own deductions. She declared, "In ten years of teaching, I'm seeing huge implications in this next generation's ability to work hard and not be expected to be handed information."

If teens aren't willing to work diligently, they'll have to be satisfied with the status quo. Excellence will be sacrificed for self-gratification. Without our help, they may naturally choose self-protection and ease rather than working to learn new skills and develop talents. Taking the easy road may result in character and hope never being firmly established in their lives.

Having a shortsighted, look-for-the-easy-way-out perspective may mean teens also don't discover their purpose. Because knowing our purpose is often the very thing to inspire effort, perseverance, and diligence. Without it, they can stay living in the culture of easy.[7]

So how can we ease our teens' transition out of the culture of easy?

1. We can evaluate our own attitude toward difficulties. What's our attitude when something is challenging? If our children see us abandon community or home projects, we won't have any credibility when speaking with them about their habit of giving up. I encourage you to process what's going on within yourself so that persevering, asking for help, and dealing with the imperfections of life get easier for you to manage.

2. We can resist the urge to rescue our kids from hard experiences. Are you allowing your kids to give up too frequently or too soon rather than working with them? Ideally while in our homes, our kids learn how to view obstacles optimistically and gain experience in overcoming them. Let them know the stress they feel is normal, not something to instantly run from. Tell them they'll grow and mature by learning. I totally agree with Chapman and Pellicane who wrote, "As long as that child feels secure in your love, she will thrive when challenged."[8] Without security as a firm foundation, teens' identity and competence won't grow. Without security, they'll never develop resiliency. They won't learn how to view mistakes in healthy ways, struggle without feeling stupid, or truly believe failure isn't final or fatal.[9]

3. We can help our kids persevere by teaching them and encouraging them. Rather than *telling* them what to do, we need to teach them what they need to know and do. We might be surprised by how often our kids truly don't know *how* to improve. We can make it safe for them to ask for help. Also, we can correct and not criticize. Rather than just telling them they did something well, we can *specifically* point out their strengths so they'll know to use them again.[10]

4. We can help our kids understand how God works in and through us. Share truths with your teen that will help him or her persevere in difficult tasks or experiences. Philippians 4:13 comes to mind: "I can do all things through him who gives me strength." Talk about what it means, in rubber-hits-the-road, everyday terms, to depend on God for strength. Maybe it involves praying through the process, asking others to pray for you, and meditating on Bible verses. For example, Psalm 59:17 talks about relying on God. How does that work out in real life? Do you have Bible heroes who faced tremendous difficulties and whose stories encourage or inspire you? You might read those with your teen. Talk about how faith comes into play in hard times and hard situations, despite our culture of easy.[11]

5. We can talk about the difference between joy and happiness. Happiness is dictated by our circumstances, which can change all the time. Joy is dictated by our relationship with God, who never changes. Happiness comes and goes; joy can be present in our hearts all the time.

> **Help teens** to identify the gratification of hard work.

6. We can help them understand the joy and satisfaction that comes from hard work. There's nothing better than working hard and then stepping back and saying, "I did that." My friends have a middle-schooler, D.J., who has just taken over lawn-mowing duties since his older brother left for college. D.J. drags his feet when he's asked to mow, but then he seems quite proud of the job well done once he's finished. My friends notice D.J.'s satisfaction with his growing maturity and responsibility; he's pleased to be doing what used to be the "big kids' job." My friends openly remark on that feeling and commend his work, hoping to reinforce D.J.'s own pleasure in tackling big jobs. When you see teens working hard and accomplishing something, call attention to the internal satisfaction they feel upon accomplishment. Help them to identify the gratification of hard work.

7. We can talk about living life to the fullest. This is a fantastic age in which we can document our lives and history in unprecedented ways. But to truly live, to experience the full joy of the moment, we have to be free from our screens and remember our lives were never meant to be contained in 140 characters or fewer. The more you invest in relationships in real time, the more your kids will be likely to follow your example.

We Live in a Culture of Entertainment

The culture of entertainment is all around us. As Jill Savage and I addressed in *No More Perfect Kids,* teens who use tech toys frequently may incorrectly conclude they must be entertained in order to be happy.[12] Since they view happiness as their right, by extension many see entertainment as their right. Even those who don't play games on their devices pick up from peers how much fun all their technology is. To be honest, gaming is genuinely fun for a lot of people. However, it is detrimental if their demand for "fun" increases the likelihood they'll avoid work, including daily chores and responsibilities.

When we hear kids talking about wanting to be entertained, we need to understand it's usually not people who entertain them. Rather, they're entertained by fast-paced and challenging activities and stimulating content. I've been saying for years that it's engagement they actually want, not entertainment. Many youth tell me the entertainment culture in some youth groups is insulting. They don't want to be entertained for the sake of being entertained. They do want to engage with meaningful content.

The slow pace and lack of challenge are major reasons school frustrates so many of our youth. The dropout rate is stunning—8.1 percent of high school students do not graduate, 8,300 drop out each day, and 36 percent of those dropouts are ninth graders. They're making early decisions to not complete school.[13] Of the many who go on to college, 46 percent do not earn a degree, even after attending for six years.[14]

Getting past the need for constant entertainment is relevant for working teens, too, and for those beginning to think about their future. Whether they're helping out at home or working, it's not realistic for them to think all jobs will be entertaining and stimulating. When jobs are tedious or require long hours of concentration or physical effort, kids may give up. Apathy sets in. When listening to us talk about our jobs, what do they learn? Often that's a great place for us to start when thinking about how our teens perceive environments that aren't entertaining or interesting.

1. We can provide a list of activities they can do that don't involve technology. Because most teens hate being bored, we can brainstorm with them some non-tech activity ideas. The numbered list can be posted in a convenient place. They can refer to the list when they can't think of something to do. When a child complains, "I'm bored!" we can say, "Go do #17." After we use this idea a few times, and they don't like whatever random number we choose (that might have been "Do your laundry"), they might complain less often about being bored.

2. We can encourage non-tech activities in everyday life. When driving in the car, you might randomly comment about what's outside the windows, maybe considering your particular teens' interests: "Whoa! The architecture in this neighborhood is really varied. Do you think we can guess just by looking which decade each house was designed in?" or "What kind of tree do you think that is?" You might play word games, guessing games, or storytelling games in the car. You could leave a cool puzzle out on a card table for family members to work on as they have time. If you're at the library, pick up heavily illustrated books on subjects that will probably interest your kids and leave them lying around your living room or family room. Make it easy for them to "dawdle" over something other than their screens.

3. We can talk with our kids about the value of being bored. Boredom is a fact of life and can't always be avoided. Teach your children how to deal with boredom, rather than always trying to avoid it. Talk with them about being alone with their thoughts, about the benefits of quiet, and about choosing sometimes to rest in solitude. Explain how times of mental inactivity is actually healthy for their brains and their emotions.

We Live in a Culture of New

The culture of new also keeps teens happy. Many parents buy them the newest and best of everything, often on the first day it comes out. For example, 3.2 million DVD Blu-Ray Discs of the movie *Frozen* were sold on the first day it was released.[15] Sales of the video game *Call of Duty: Ghosts* exceeded $1 billion on its first day.[16] Just because we can afford to buy something doesn't mean we should. Sometimes teaching our children the value of delayed gratification will actually serve them better than any DVD we give them on its release date.

The culture of new that tells us we need the latest and greatest breeds serious discontentment. Just because something is old doesn't mean it should be replaced. Before purchasing my current smartphone, I had a "dumb phone," a plain cellphone. It wasn't the latest and greatest, and my nieces enjoyed pointing that out. But it worked. It did what I needed my cellphone to do. I was satisfied, but frequently had to defend my decision. In their book *Living with Less So Your Family Has More*, Mark and Jill Savage share a story about not having an HD television. No one in the family complained until they experienced HDTV in a vacation rental home. Suddenly their old TV didn't seem as good. The Savage family did not get a new television, but they did get a quick lesson in how easily discontent can creep in.[17]

Some teachers have mentioned to me how more and more children won't use broken crayons in school. They throw them away as soon as the paper comes off or the crayons break. I still remember the large plastic container of broken crayons my second-grade students enjoyed digging through when they were lacking a particular color. There is something fulfilling about using resources well and appreciating their value. It's important for us to help teens be content with function and not live in the discontent of not having everything "new."

So how can we help teens keep from buying into the culture of new?

1. We can resist the urge to buy them whatever they want.
We may, however, let them earn and save up to buy things they'd
like to have after they've worked for it. We can help them learn
to manage their money.[18] It's great training for teens to explain
and defend their desire to spend money—yours or their own—
on some new technology or tool. Our ensuing conversation will
allow us to reinforce values, teach decision-making and thinking
skills, establish priorities, and define tech as a tool and not a right.

2. We can say no when it's appropriate. A parental no can
drive a teen to creative solutions. We help them succeed by teaching them to save up. We can help them value what they've already
got by encouraging them to donate an old toy or video game every
time they buy or receive a new one. We can value their outgrown
tools and toys the same way we value their outgrown clothes—by
giving them away to someone who needs or values them. When
they can't just discard old things, they revisit the value of those
items—and that can cultivate gratitude in their hearts.

**3. We can help them recognize the temporary "buzz"
from getting something new.** How long a gap is there between
"I've just got to have this or that!" to "Oh, that old thing! Now I
need this instead"? Help your kids notice that some of the stuff
now relegated to the back of their closets once gave them an
amazing feeling of great satisfaction. Point out how short a time
those feelings of gratification last. As Chapman and Pellicane remind us in *Growing Up Social,* "The kind of happiness that comes
from acquiring things is temporary at best. We do children a great

disservice when we give them everything they want. This is not how the real world works."[19]

We Live in a Culture of Restart

The culture of restart is a teen's default mode. Partly because the "culture of new" influences them, they'd rather restart something than repair it. Those of us who are older are willing to try to repair broken things. How many times have I pounded my rake back together after the end flew off with the leaves I tossed into a pile? Far too many to count!

Technology has taught teens that many things appear to fix themselves with just a restart. We can unplug, or power down, the device. Then, after a short waiting period, we can power back up, and it magically works. Hooray for the quick-fix reboot! I'm so glad this works! However, it seems to be sending our teens a false message that there are never any truly serious consequences. It's as if nothing *really* breaks.

Because of the culture of restart, many teens don't fully understand consequences. They don't see any consequences when their technology reboots. So they may think there aren't any consequences when they make certain decisions or mistakes in relationships or careers that force a restart. But there often are. Heartache can last a long time. For example, a teen may make a throwaway comment on social media, only to find that it offends a friend or finds its way to someone who could be hurt by it. The damage can be done before a post can be removed—and the relationship damage can't be undone by clicking "Undo."

Many young people believe they can edit or completely delete problems, much like they can improve or delete pictures taken with their phones. They can choose to not post a picture of the one negative encounter at a party. Now it's as if it never happened, out of sight and out of mind.

Teens who pretend mistakes don't happen and problems don't exist without an easy answer may never ask for help or they may refuse it when help is offered. Therefore, problems may continue and grow. Learning won't occur.

Parents can help teens acclimate to real-world consequences and cause and effect.

1. We can help our children understand consequences. We can allow our children to feel the natural or parental consequences of their poor choices. Talk about cause-effect relationships and look for teachable moments to demonstrate that some things break and can't always be restarted, repaired easily, or repaired at all. If you tell your daughter she won't be allowed to attend any social functions on the weekend if her room isn't tidied by then, don't cave in and let her go anyway when the room is a wreck and she is tearfully begging. If you've got a policy of matching gaming time with reading hours, stick to the policy and insist the game stops when the teen's "minutes" are used up.

2. We can allow our teens to take responsibility for their actions. Sometimes the "easy fix" capabilities of technology may lead them to *not* see their own culpabilities when things go wrong in life and relationships. Watch for this and don't let them live in denial. Talk about how words and actions hurt people's hearts. Talk about invisible wounds. It's not about punishment, although that may sometimes be appropriate. It's more about allowing natural consequences to fall into place and us choosing to not rescue our kids from the need to take personal responsibility. For example, if our teens are mean to their peers—say, sending bully-type texts or posting private information as social media updates—they may not be invited to hang out with others. They won't be trusted. If they're caught cheating on a test, they won't be left alone while studying to make sure they take it seriously and they will be separated and carefully observed during the next test. If they spend more time gaming than they're allowed to, they lose the privilege to game for a designated period of time. These types of consequences help teens learn cause and effect and that not everything can just be "restarted."

3. We can use our words to help them connect the dots between cause and effect. An effective way to promote personal responsibility is to use phrases such as "Your bullying texts *caused* your friends to ignore you." "*Your decision* means you lose computer privileges." "*You chose* to ignore what I asked you to do that you said you would do." If our teens complain, we just repeat the phrases *you caused* and *your decision* and *you chose*. Of course, similar phrases work to affirm our teens' wise decisions: "*You chose* to turn off the Wii as soon as you heard the timer go off. Thanks for that!" or "*Your decision* honored your younger brother. Way to go!"

We Live in a Culture of Entitlement

Many parents—and teachers and employers!—complain about the culture of entitlement. Entitlement causes teens to want what they want when they want it, without having to work for it, and sometimes just because everybody else has it. Their pursuit of happiness is fueled by entitlement. Also, entitled kids want others to fix their problems and clean up their messes. They don't take responsibility for themselves and they want to be treated as the exception to the rule.

Erin Long blogged about "6 Small Habits to Increase Contentment when Life Isn't Easy": "Our sense of entitlement can hold us back from embracing the beauty in our lives and seeing the blessings that are in front of us. We experience contentment when we choose to reframe how we look at our circumstances and ground our expectations in reality."[20]

> **We can help** our teens understand the difference between wants and needs.

Parents take the leading role in breaking their teens' sense of entitlement. Here are some ways to help.

1. We can examine our own attitudes. Do our teens hear us complain about it not being fair that we don't have the latest and greatest tablet or gadget after seeing a "cool" commercial? Do we appear to resent colleagues who have bigger offices or newer phones even though they earned them? Have we appeared to place our security, and even our identity, in what we think we should own? If so, ask God to reveal the lessons you can learn and with humility (and as appropriate) pass those lessons on to your children. If your role modeling wasn't exactly great along these lines in the past, own it, and explain how you are making adjustments.

2. We can help our teens understand the difference between wants and needs. It's a key to making sure their core needs are met in healthy ways. If life is always about what they want, they'll never be satisfied or content. God didn't design us to be satisfied by things or to place our security in our stuff. If you've learned that the hard way, be vulnerable and honest with your kids. It helps if we're careful how we use the words *want* and *need.* We can correct our kids when they use the wrong word and we can ask them to help us in the same way. It may be a habit we need to break. Do we *need* a cup of coffee or *want* one? Do we *need* to text a friend or do we *want* to? Also, we can think about how we ask them to help us. Do we *want* them to empty the dishwasher or do we *need* them to? Do we *want* them to carry clean clothes upstairs or do we *need* them to?

3. We can cultivate thankfulness. Thankfulness balances out entitlement. Any gift that our kids are given should be acknowledged with a handwritten thank-you note that's put in the mail. This slows down life and lets our kids be reminded that their gifts aren't "deserved" but rather a blessing. They acknowledge the time, money, and effort given by the gift-giver. If you're not in the habit of writing thank-you notes, start with yourself and encourage your kids to do the same. Instill that attitude of gratitude. Being truly grateful increases humility, contentment, and joy.

Sometimes teens feel more thankful when they've been exposed to children and teens who have less than they do. I remember watching children in the slums of Africa happily kicking rocks back and forth. There was no entitlement there! Those kids didn't know to wish for what they didn't know they didn't have. They appeared content to focus on that day and their reality. When you see people enjoying what they have or content in their circumstances, mention it to your teens. Draw their attention to the joy that comes with gratitude and contentment.

4. We can model our dependence on God's provision. We need to articulate for teens what it means to ask God for our "daily bread." Have you ever thought about the words at the beginning of the Lord's Prayer? Matthew 6:11 reads, "Give us today our daily bread." I've had meaningful discussions with teens and young adults about why Jesus taught His disciples—and that's us, too!—to ask for just our *daily* bread. Depending on God for what we need today helps us battle entitlement as we increase our trust in God's provision and pursue joy rather than happiness.

5. We can modify our gift-giving. To combat entitlement, many parents give just three gifts to each child at Christmas—something to wear, something for fun, and something educational. They also ask grandparents to not go overboard. Giving fewer gifts, together with helping teens give toys and clothes away when they're getting new ones, can keep the focus off ourselves and on others. These could be changes we make as a family or changes we implement as legitimate consequences for our teens' demanding, complaining, I'm-never-satisfied attitudes. Living from a selfless default is much more rewarding than a self-centered approach to life. We just have to help our kids discover this.

We Live in a Culture of Winning

Have you observed the culture of winning in your teens? Combined with the culture of entitlement, they expect higher and higher rewards each time they play. They expect to win regularly, too! Winning can be so important that children restart some games because they can't risk losing. Especially for gamers, this high-speed-equals-high-rewards culture is a huge contributor to living out the happiness lie.

Because playing often makes higher scores realistic, some teens conclude that doing well is only a factor of time, but not talent, skill, or effort. This is why it can be challenging and stressful to truly need to rely on talent, skill, or effort when studying, practicing a musical instrument, memorizing Bible verses, and the like.

Have you noticed teens' need for instant feedback and instant gratification? Gaming can be a factor. Games automatically keep score and often light up or vibrate when certain feats are accomplished. Our young people are conditioned to know immediately how well they're doing. Many parents, grandparents, and teachers have told me kids expect lots of feedback and it can be time-consuming and challenging to keep them satisfied. When teens don't know where they stand in the real world, some have told me they get nervous, insecure, and distracted. They have a need to keep score. For some, scoring points is like a drug fix.[21]

Think about this: Playing games that keep score makes self-evaluation unnecessary. Our kids don't have to take a minute to ask themselves how they are doing. They don't need to reflect on their efforts. Many teachers have told me more and more students are asking for immediate feedback with a demanding tone when turning in their work. When teachers ask how they think they did, they hear things like, "I don't know. You haven't graded it yet."

> **In time, we** want teens not to look to our voice to affirm or correct them but rather to learn to hear God's voice for guidance and feedback.

How can parents help their kids get over the idea that they need to win?

1. We can help our teens learn to evaluate their own work. We can provide specific feedback about the process they used and the product they achieved. Ideally, we provide it after they tell us how they think they did and why. This can increase their ability to self-evaluate. Eventually they need to become less dependent on technology, teachers, and us, and decide for themselves if they're satisfied with how they did. So, although they want us to tell them how they did and may need us to at the beginning of this transition, let's stand our ground and tell them less often so they learn to trust their inner voice. In time, we want them not to look to our voice to affirm or correct them but rather to learn to hear God's voice for guidance and feedback (John 14:26).

2. We can give presence rather than praise. Maria Popova wrote a fascinating piece about the importance of prioritizing presence over praise when our goal is a child's achievement. Although her illustration involves a four-year-old boy, the result may be true for a person of any age. Popova writes:

> I once watched Charlotte with a four-year-old boy, who was drawing. When he stopped and looked up at her—perhaps expecting praise—she smiled and said, "There is a lot of blue in your picture." He replied, "It's the pond near my grandmother's house—there is a bridge." He picked up a brown crayon, and said, "I'll show you." Unhurried, she talked to the child, but more importantly she observed, she listened. She was present.[22]

Popova writes that psychologist Stephen Grosz argues that presence "helps build the child's confidence by way of indicating he is worthy of the observer's thoughts and attention—its absence, on the other hand, divorces in the child the journey from the destination by instilling a sense that the activity itself is worthless unless it's a means to obtaining praise."[23]

Being present and directing our attention to kids can be something *better* than praise. People of all ages respond to the feeling that someone is thinking about them, focusing on them, valuing who they are and what they have to say. Tune in to your teens. Close your own laptop or iPad so you can give them your eye contact.

We Live in a Culture of "Like"

The culture of "like" is also alive and well and contributing to the pursuit of happiness. Pictures, videos, and details about teens' days can be immediately "liked" and shared through social media sites. It's more important to many to be liked in an online community than in person. They also may think it's more realistic to be liked digitally because they're not totally known—warts and all—by their online "friends." Placing an inappropriate emphasis on technology and their digital "friends" is part of the worldview lie that "I am the center of my own universe." Unfortunately, for many, being paid attention to is more important than paying attention. Technology allows for endless self-promotion. It's become the adult version of show-and-tell.[24] What happens may feel like true belonging, but it's often not.

When you were in high school, how did you know if you were "cool"? Maybe popular students asked you to sit with them at lunch or tucked invitations into your hallway locker. Maybe someone else would notice that. As Sarah Brooks points out, "There may have been a few eyewitnesses and it was pure joy."[25]

A major difference for our kids today is that their popularity status can be determined by a numerical value provided by their peers. They can rank themselves. Brooks writes, "Let me explain . . . Your daughter has 139 followers, which is twenty-three fewer than Jessica, but fifty-six more than Beau. Your son's photo had thirty-eight likes which was fourteen fewer than Travis's photo, but twenty-two more than Spencer's."[26] As she points out, there's less mystery. Today's teens can't assume they are or aren't popular based on face-to-face interactions like we did. Popularity is now quantifiable and explicit.

Young people have probably always had a tendency to pay more attention to themselves than to others. It's just easier for today's youth to be self-centered because of the constant connection and temptation technology provides. For instance, rather than perusing Facebook to see who and what they can like, they hover over their own posts to see who has liked them. Some teens unfriend peers who don't like their posts often enough.

A friend of a friend recently talked with her former education professor. She asked how things were going and the professor commented on his concern for his students, all of whom intended to become teachers one day. He explained that he had students take out their phones on the first day of class. He instructed

> **We can teach** teens that character and talent are more important than simply receiving online affirmation.

them to take a picture—and 85 percent of them took selfies. He fears they won't make very good teachers if they don't change that attitude. I absolutely agree!

Parents also want to shift their teens from self-centeredness. What can we do to help?

1. We can increase opportunities for self-evaluation. Help your kids to evaluate their efforts without counting "likes" or looking for social media feedback. Talk about what they learned in the process or what they discovered about themselves as they worked on a project. We can affirm and edify intrinsic value that God put within our children in healthy and appropriate ways. We can teach them that character and talent are more important than simply receiving online affirmation.

2. We can be careful of our own responses to the "like" factor. When we post an update on Facebook or a picture on Instagram, do we watch to see how long it takes before someone likes it? Do I believe my blog is worth reading, but question myself a day after posting it because it wasn't liked or shared enough? Do I forget how often I read things, like them, but don't click on the "like" button to give feedback? Might people do that with my blog, too? Online approval, silence, or rejection might inform, but it should never be the barometer of intrinsic value.

> **Find healthy** and appropriate ways to notice and affirm what you value in your teen.

3. We can affirm and edify our teens' intrinsic value. Each teen has been created by God, in His image—and the sacrifice of Jesus was made to purchase each teen's life for God. So our teens have intrinsic value—and unique gifts and personalities (Psalm 139). We can find healthy and appropriate ways to notice and affirm what we value in our teens. We can teach them that character and talent are more important than simply receiving online affirmation.

4. We can make sure our kids are familiar with growth points in their lives. Especially if our children are active on social media, we should make sure they're aware of their weaknesses so they can learn and be strengthened as a result. It's not that they should post about their faults, but by posting only about their strengths, or victories on the football field or volleyball court, and other successes, they can forget they have weaknesses to improve and challenges to overcome. This may cause them to plateau and maintain an unrealistic view of themselves. Make sure they know talking with God about their weaknesses isn't shaming, but wise (Hebrews 4:15). Developing an attitude like Paul's is mature. He wrote in 2 Corinthians 12:9, "But he [Jesus] said to me, 'My grace is sufficient for you, for my power is made perfect in weakness.' Therefore I will boast all the more gladly about my weaknesses, so that Christ's power may rest on me."

5. We can help teens process their emotions well. Some teens post cryptic messages that may be attempts to dodge parental or outsiders understanding, but they may also be cries for help. Some never post anything negative. In both cases, they may be stuffing a lot that we could help them think through. Be available. Be present. If you experience their quick temper or they seem easily frustrated, there may be something going on under the surface. Be the parent and create opportunities to talk and connect.[27]

6. We can decrease media time and increase tech-free time. One sure way of dealing well with the "like" factor is to spend less time on social media and more time in face-to-face real-time interactions. Encourage your kids to be involved in activities where iron can truly sharpen iron (Proverbs 27:17) and they can experience the "living water" of life-giving relationships with Christ and others.

THE TRUTH WE WANT TEENS TO BELIEVE

Parents can feel overwhelmed as they try to counterbalance the influences of the culture of now, impatience, easy, entertainment, new, entitlement, winning, and like. Whew! But we can't lose heart! Our teens need us to keep on pouring truth into their lives, by word and example.

What's the truth we want teens to believe instead of this lie that they deserve to be happy all the time? It comes down to understanding the difference between happiness and joy. The truth is that happiness is short-term and joy is long-term. Happiness is externally influenced, and joy is internal. We deserve nothing, and yet God has given us everything: Himself. Being grateful continually rather than needing to be happy constantly shows maturity.

Internal joy, peace, and contentment, which are all possible no matter my circumstances, are wise to pursue through a dynamic relationship with Jesus Christ.

We can direct today's young people away from the pursuit of happiness toward the pursuit of something more lasting—joy. This will cultivate gratefulness and increase contentment in their hearts. Joy, gratefulness, and contentment will serve them well in marriage, work, and the relationships that mean the most.

Lie #2: I deserve to be happy all the time.
Truth #2: I can have joy no matter my circumstances.

The joy of the Lord is your strength.
Nehemiah 8:10

6

LIE #3: I MUST HAVE CHOICES

When teaching parents and teachers about the effects of technology on teens, I almost always ask, "How many of your teens complain and argue way more than you thought they would?" As they audibly moan, practically the whole audience raises their hands. When they see many hands in the air, they're encouraged to discover they're not alone.

Parents are encouraged again as they learn that the complaints are not necessarily indica-

Variety is their spice of life, and multiple available choices mean that change is constant.

tive of ineffective parenting but can be directly linked to technology use.

Teens are surrounded by choice! In technologically developed nations, we're privileged with more options than we can handle. Because young people have never known life without many choices, their brains are wired to expect options. Being given a choice is an automatic preference. Choice is one of the things that keeps them happy so this lie is related to the happiness lie. Variety is their spice of life, and multiple available choices mean that change is constant.

Just when we figured out that a teen likes a certain brand of jeans, a particular band, the youth group at the church we just checked out, or a sandwich at the deli on the corner, he changes his mind. She changes her mind about future career possibilities as often as she changes her favorite song, her favorite kind of car, or the color of her nail polish. It's not that teens have stopped liking the things they liked yesterday; they just like to change things up and keep their options open. They know that at any moment, they might like something else better. And most teens think they *need* this range of options.

Deep down, teens long for a connection with you.

Let's find out how much this lie is influencing your teens' behavior and yours. Remember, because young people's beliefs are heavily influenced by who they listen to, it's your job as a parent to pursue relationship with them so you can talk about these things. Connect through technology and without it. Listen. Watch. Talk. Listen some more.[1] Deep down, they long for a connection with you.

EVIDENCE OF THE LIE:
REASONS WHY AND THINGS TO TRY

Teens believe they need choice and that choices are their right for two primary reasons: the variety of options always available to them and the drop-down menus used by so many technology tools, toys, and services. For some kids, there's a third cause. If they have premature freedom to make decisions and they regularly do what they want, freedom of choice will be their expectation. So, if we've prioritized happiness to keep the peace, and recognize we've contributed to the culture of "I don't want that, I want this," let's own it and talk about it with our teens as we work to improve our relationship and their future.

Of course technology has contributed to this lie being believed by many, many young people. We've already established how prevalent choice is. For example, in one minute Instagram users post 216,000 new photos and YouTube users upload 72 hours of new video.[2] You read that right—every minute we have 72 more hours of video to choose from. Spotify allows us to choose from among more than 20 million songs and iTunes Radio has more than 27 million.[3] There are almost 1 billion websites.[4] It's no wonder teens believe they deserve choices!

Choice shows up everywhere. Like me, you may remember a time when there were just a few restaurants near your home. Going out to eat might have been a rare treat. In contrast, many of our children have eaten out often. Not only that, but think how the number of choices at these restaurants has increased over the years. For instance, where I live, Mexican food is especially popular. It's rare that a non-Mexican restaurant doesn't serve their version of something Mexican. Just thinking about the options at my local coffee bar makes my head spin.

There's another contrast with the "old days" relevant to this lie. When I was a teen, biblical morality was the norm. There was great consistency in a community, and even in our country, as to what constituted right and wrong. This naturally decreased options and limited choice. Of course, not everybody thought then or thinks now that this is a good thing. However, we can't deny that it narrowed choices.

When a teacher assigned a paper of 300 words due Tuesday, we wrote a paper that long and turned it in on Tuesday. When a youth pastor said permission slips needed to be turned in the Saturday before camp, we knew to turn ours in by then if we wanted to go. When a parent or grandparent asked us to help with the dishes, it would have been unthinkable to beg off or suggest someone else help instead.

> **As appealing** as choices are, and as necessary as teens believe they are, too much of a good thing isn't always a good thing.

What emotional responses are you having to these illustrations? Do you relate to a different time, or do you relate more to this generation of choices? Now that we've identified several lies, perhaps you're beginning to predict which of your teens' beliefs and behaviors are related to this lie. Let's find out more about this demand for choice and how it's affecting teens.

Many Teens Are Overwhelmed

As appealing as choices are, and as necessary as teens believe they are, too much of a good thing isn't always a good thing. Consider this. I have so many CDs on my desk that I sometimes don't want to have to decide which one to listen to so I turn on the radio instead. I let the producer of that show make decisions for me. (Yes, it's true: I still use ancient technology called "a CD Player." I paid for my CDs, my CD player still works, so I use them.) When it comes to too many choices, paralysis rather than liberation is a common occurrence.[5]

So how can we help young people maintain equilibrium when they are inundated with so many choices they could be overwhelmed?

1. We can help our teens know that it's okay to change their minds sometimes. Many teens want to make right decisions and are afraid they'll be wrong or they'll change their mind. We can explain that changing their mind doesn't mean they were wrong or they failed. It's often the case that what is right today isn't going to be right a month from now. Maybe the situation changed, or we've gained better information about people or a situation. Rethinking a decision doesn't always mean the first decision was wrong.

2. We can provide helpful feedback so choosing doesn't seem so overwhelming. We can help teens think through *why* a choice was wise or not. If it was unwise, was it because the choice was dangerous, selfish, immature, or lazy? We can help them analyze their wise decisions, too. What past experiences guided them to a smart choice? Did they integrate your feedback into their thinking? Were they efficient, creative, or something else? We can also help them anticipate how similar thinking could be relevant to future decisions.

3. We can limit choices when possible. Because they are forced to make so many choices all the time, we can help them narrow down choices when possible. We might do this when looking at colleges or choosing classes at school. Rather than looking at all the options in front of them, narrow the choices to some of the best options for them. Talk about simple ways to disqualify options to make some choices easier.

Dissatisfaction creeps in because teens have so many good options constantly available to them.

Many Teens Are Dissatisfied

After dealing with being overwhelmed, teens finally choose. But, as psychologist Barry Schwartz explains, "Whenever you're choosing one thing, you're choosing not to do other things. And those other things may have lots of attractive features, and it's going to make what you're doing less attractive."[6] Dissatisfaction creeps in because teens have so many good options constantly available to them.

We've already recognized that teens can be stressed and prone to depression. Being overwhelmed and second-guessing decisions can cause stress. Making choices that line up with the other lies we've established will also result in eventual dissatisfaction.

Remember Lie #1, that each person is the center of his or her own universe? Because of their worldview, everything is supposed to be about today's teens. But making choices that always leave them at the center of the wheel can also leave them lonely and frustrated when others don't respond as if they're the center. They may try to be the center of their own universe, but they can't be the center of everybody else's. Cue dissatisfaction and even anger.

Lie #2—that teens have to be happy all the time—plays into dissatisfaction, too. Choosing so they're happy all the time gets exhausting. Being self-centered and selfish in this regard certainly puts others off, which can lead straight to loneliness. And, when it looks like they shouldn't be lonely, based on the number of "friends" in their networks and on their phone, it's even worse.

It's also very possible that prioritizing happiness means teens won't develop emotional resiliency. They may not stick around and process disappointment and unhappiness in healthy ways. Rather, they'll just make a new decision they're sure will result in happiness. It's a vicious cycle of disappointment and discouragement.

So how can we direct teens to more satisfying patterns of handling choices?

1. We must model and teach criteria and standards that are better than happiness and healthier than "It's all about me." Satisfying choices are based on core values that guide our decision-making. The Bible can help us make choices that line up with our biblical beliefs and honor God. Family values can drive our choices. Sometimes predetermined priorities or boundaries guide our decisions. For instance, if you decide ahead of time that you will not carry more than two volunteer responsibilities at a time, it makes the decision simpler when you're faced with a third option. Either you step away from something you're already doing to take on the new volunteer position or you decline the new option.

2. We can help teens understand the *why's*. For our children to use healthy criteria in decision-making, they'll need to understand the good reasons we have for choosing those healthy parameters. We shouldn't assume the why's are obvious or that the reasons we value what we value are obvious. Most often, the *why* isn't seen or heard. To pass on our values, we must talk about them often,[7] encourage our children to observe us, and not assume every question they ask is judgmental. We can use those teachable moments that happen in the throes of life to explain why we just did what we did. Having them contribute to a family mission statement of sorts that outlines how decisions are made could be very helpful as well.

3. We can provide helpful, consistent, and specific observations about who teens are. When young people know themselves well, they'll be better able to choose what's best for them. But they often don't know themselves well yet.[8] We can help them by giving specific feedback as we have opportunity. "You were very patient last night. I know that because you answered your sister's questions when you were helping her with her homework. I'm proud of you for being helpful and patient." If it appears that your teen doesn't care what you think, don't give up! This is an important part of developing security and identity in their developing hearts.

Serving others is a sure way of learning more about ourselves.

4. We can give teens opportunity to serve. Serving others is a sure way of learning more about ourselves. When doing something for others, teens will be stretched in their personal strength and competence. This can be as simple as taking an elderly relative to a doctor's appointment, helping a teacher after school, or helping another homeschooling family with a project. Or it might be as big as a church-sponsored, multi-day missions trip, or feeding the poor. They might discover what fulfills them and what causes joy to bubble up. Self-awareness can help them make healthier choices.

5. We can give teens opportunities to consider others. Serving can motivate teens to consider others when making choices and decisions. Putting others first can become very satisfying when it's experienced often enough. Just recently, a young girl who purchased school supplies for others declared loudly to her mom, "That felt good, mommy! Let's do it again!" As Christ role-modeled for us, selflessness and sacrificial service facilitates real growth, honest relationship, and not despair or isolation. Doing projects like sponsoring and communicating with a Compassion International child, or filling a shoebox for Operation Christmas Child, or selecting, wrapping, and delivering a Project Angel Tree gift can help teens consider others and factor others into their choices.

Both successes and failures result in emotions that have to be handled with maturity.

6. We can find opportunities to teach emotional resiliency. We need to help our teens process disappointment and joy in healthy ways. We can help them understand, believe, and act upon the reality that people deal with emotions differently and there's no one right way. We can talk about times we did and did not handle things well—and how we dealt with that emotionally, for good or bad. Using characters in literature or television, Bible heroes, or inventors or explorers they're studying in school, we can discuss how others responded emotionally to dissatisfaction, disappointment, and discouragement—the dangerous Ds! We can do the same when teaching about handling life graciously and with humility when our choices and decisions turn out great.

Both successes and failures result in emotions that have to be handled with maturity.

7. We can raise the call to contentment. Contentment, regardless of circumstance, is a beautiful thing to hold up to our teens as a realistic expectation and something to strive for. It's possible when the five core needs are met in God. Contentment is found in us, not around us. We can't buy it or perform it. Being satisfied or dissatisfied with this choice or that shouldn't rock our world. Contentment feels safe and solid, because it is a safe and solid state of being.

8. We can determine if we're giving teens unnecessary choices. Courageously analyze what's been going on lately in your home. Are we feeding dissatisfaction and discontent by always giving our kids a choice when it's not necessary or appropriate? How can we help them discover and believe choice is a privilege, not a right? If they don't learn this in the safety of our homes, they may never be satisfied because they'll always be thinking there was something else they could have thought, done, felt, or become. I've encouraged parents to "take back" the kitchen and stop making multiple options to keep various eaters happy. I tell them, "If you make meatloaf, serve meatloaf. Be the parent and not the short-order cook." Kids don't need choices at every mealtime. It's great for them to learn to be thankful for what they have. Not expecting choices at every meal is a small way you can help kids get used to going with the flow.

9. We can point teens toward God's truth about choices.
As you dig into the Bible yourself, look for passages and Bible stories that deal with issues of choices, desires, and contentment. Bring these into your family discussions or devotions. The parable of the lost son in Luke 15:11–32 might be a good place to start. There are two sons in the story who make highly discussable choices! You might check out Proverbs 30:15–30 and Ecclesiastes 6:9. If your teen is willing and a motivated learner, ask him or her to join you in the search for verses about satisfaction and dissatisfaction.

Many Teens Complain and Argue

Honestly, I could also have written that last sentence as "Many adults complain and argue." Have you noticed it? Many adults have also bought the lie we *need* choice. Add to that the ammunition of being overwhelmed and dissatisfied, and we have plenty of potential battles on our hands.

I'll admit it's sometimes easy to see what's wrong and how I was denied a better option. I hear about demanding adults everywhere I go. For example, preschool directors at a recent conference I spoke at told me that many parents are asking them to change the time for dropping off their children to something more convenient for them. "I need to drop my son off at 7:45 so I'm not late for work.

> **Teens complain** and argue because they expect options.

That will be okay with you, right?" People expect others to accommodate their personal needs, all the time!

What have we modeled before our teens? Have they heard us complain more than we express gratitude? Are we frustrated and even disgusted when a store runs out of what we wanted? (Or did we express it as a need when it was really something we just wanted?) Do we take it personally when an appointment time we wanted wasn't available or when a book from the library was checked out by someone else? How do our children see us react and treat others? What do they hear us say and not say? When things go well, what do they hear us say and not say?

Teens complain and argue because they think they "need" choice and that it's their right. They expect options. Remember, this is wired into their brains so it's not just a matter of character. When given no options or only a few and none of them are "good enough," they verbalize their discontent.

The complaining and arguing are related to the culture of entitlement, which feeds the lie that they deserve to be happy all the time. They want more options, and they want to present their own options when not given a choice. Many teachers have told me of students who suggest that doing fifteen math problems would

Real gratitude is genuine and affirming in its specificity.

be just as good as doing twenty-five and that turning something in on Wednesday would be more convenient for them. If I'd dared to have such thoughts when I was a teen, I'm pretty sure I would not have dared to verbalize them! Today's teens, however, don't hesitate to verbalize their preferences.

So how can we help young people reverse the tendency to complain and argue?

1. We can evaluate our own complaining and arguing. Do we constantly complain? Do our teens know we use social media to mention how badly we were treated at this store and how dismissed we felt during a particular encounter? Is nothing right with the world? There's no perfect church, school, curriculum, or neighborhood? No government official does anything right? The prices are too high! The traffic is terrible! Negativity is contagious. We are hypocrites if we ask (or strongly suggest) they should change their attitudes and just accept things as they are when they hardly see us do the same.

2. We can be truly grateful and express it regularly. We have much to be thankful for. All of us do. You may be getting tired of my constant returning to the solution of gratitude, but gratefulness is a definite answer to so many of the problems that concern us and concern young people! Real gratitude is not a fake "thank you" spoken because it's the right thing we have to do. Real gratitude is genuine and affirming in its specificity.

3. We can help our teens be discerning about advertising messages. Teaching young people to discern what's really going on in advertising can help them become less demanding and argumentative about needing a particular game or app.

Show them and teach them, using print advertising and television ads, about bias, manipulative language, outright lies, stereotypes, and the use of objectification and sex to sell everything.[9] Explain that we should all have more respect for ourselves so we're not sucked into the manipulative and often demeaning way of thinking some companies want us to use. Consumer-conscious teens may argue less about things they want because they'll intelligently evaluate the messages that come at them.

But disagreeing must be done respectfully and with evidence that teens know your role and theirs.

4. We can practice not getting sucked into teens' arguments and complaints. When teens are in a disagreeable, argumentative stage, there are three ways parents can respond well. One is to not enter the conversation so it becomes a debate. Debate is what they want. They've perhaps learned how to push your buttons and get you to add the option they want you to include when discussing Saturday or Sunday's plans. So either remain silent, calmly repeat what you've heard them say, or say something like "I hear you." Stand your ground, and they might walk off mumbling something like, "Okay, okay, I'll do it your way."

A second response that can work when they're complaining is to directly and calmly ask, "How may I help you decide?" This implies you will help but you're finished with the whiny, complaining, I-don't-want-to attitude. Whining doesn't solve any problems. After they make a statement or ask a question in a respectful tone, help them as you can.

A third response is to make sure you've stated your expectation clearly. Then, if the arguing begins, simply state, "I love you too much to argue with you." Then, if it's safe, remove yourself from their presence. Depending on their age and the circumstances, you can add, "When you calm down and think about this, come find me." Arguing isn't healthy or helpful. It's not what loving people do. It doesn't mean we can't disagree. But disagreeing must be done respectfully and with evidence that teens know your role and theirs.

5. We can help teens become aware of God's teaching about complaining and arguing. Searching for applicable Bible verses could be very helpful. Not only are there relevant Proverbs, but Old Testament and New Testament heroes provide rich instruction. Remember those one-another verses? They apply here, too: "Don't grumble against one another" (James 5:9) and "Live in peace with each other" (1 Thessalonians 5:13).

> **Because of** choice and teens' preference to multitask, focus is fragmented.

Many Teens Multitask and May Struggle to Focus

Teens have grown up multitasking, and many find it a struggle to stay focused. Having a choice and something else to do makes it easy to avoid what's unpleasant, hard, boring, or irrelevant. Multitasking keeps teens happy. They can avoid what they don't like. If one thing isn't meeting their needs, they can jump to something else. They jump from screen to screen, app to app, and they hop between games, movies, books, assignments, conversations, tasks, music, and so much more. They'll open another web browser tab, post another picture, comment on social media posts, and anything else to avoid boredom, waiting, or tasks they don't want to tackle.

Because of choice and their preference to multitask, focus is fragmented. Many admit to thinking about one thing while doing another. They don't want to get bored, and they don't like having to persevere. Finishing can be challenging.

Evidence exists to suggest multitasking isn't as common as "continuous partial attention." Teens aren't actually doing two or three things at the same time even though we think they are when we look at what's in front of them. Rather, these teens are in a constant state of partial attention. Linda Stone, a former software executive for Microsoft, writes:

> Like so many things, in small doses, continuous partial attention can be a very functional behavior. However, in large doses, it contributes to a stressful lifestyle, to operating in crisis management mode, and to a compromised ability to reflect, to make decisions, and to think creatively. In a 24/7, always-on world, continuous partial attention used as our

dominant attention mode contributes to a feeling of over-whelm, over-stimulation and to a sense of being unfulfilled. We are so accessible, we're inaccessible. The latest, greatest powerful technologies have contributed to our feeling increasingly powerless.[10]

Whether truly multitasking, which Linda Stone explains is something we do when "we are motivated by a desire to be more productive and more efficient"[11] or in the state of continuous partial attention, teens' reading, writing, comprehension, and accuracy are sacrificed. This might be fine when surveying social network feeds and some news or sports stories they stumble upon. It's not a wise or mature way to approach schoolwork or problem-solving. Approaching any assignment in these ways will have negative ramifications. Some students may earn the same grade whether focused on one thing or not. But it will take longer for them to complete their work and long-term retention may suffer.

When we model that people who are present are more important than the texts or calls we receive, we help our kids learn to make choices in favor of relationships.

How can parents help young people keep from fragmenting as they attempt to multitask too much?

1. We can address multitasking in relation to character and respect. Talking about this in terms of stewardship of time may be helpful. For example, if a teen is texting while he or she is sitting next to Grandpa, that's disrespectful to Grandpa. Texting while driving would be highly disrespectful of the value of life, considering the well-documented statistics about dangers.

2. We can model self-restraint by resisting the urge to answer calls and texts while we are with our teens. When we model that people who are present are more important than the texts or calls we receive, we help our kids learn to make choices in favor of relationships.

Many Teens Find Major Decisions Difficult

Many teens find the big, major decisions especially hard to make. Do you know high school students unable to choose a future plan—college, military, career, family? Do you know some not in college who were accepted to more than one? Do you know teens who are not dating? Not sure if they want to date? What about kids who can't decide what sport to try out for and whether to join the debate team or not? Do they wait so long trying to make up their mind that the choice is made for them? It can be so frustrating! What's going on?

For many young people who struggle to make decisions, the lies are colliding. Teens want to be happy while they're the center of the universe. They want to have choice, but choosing one thing means they can't choose something else. And they can't know

now if they'll be happy if they've never gone to college before, played basketball in high school, or dated Ashley or Jamie. As a result, they make no decision. And no decision *is* a decision.

Big decisions are challenging. They're intimidating and scary. Complex decisions definitely cause stress for many. When we talk about these decisions with our teens and let them know we're displeased with their indecisiveness, they'll be more stressed and may even become frustrated and angry. It can be a perfect storm.

> **Young people** who know who they are will be more confident when making decisions.

This is a tough area for parents, who usually have strong opinions and feelings about what they want their teens to choose. How can we help them tackle big decisions?

1. We can keep helping our kids discover their purpose and identity. Young people who know who they are and some of the reasons God created them that way will be more confident when making decisions.

2. We can provide reassurance that sometimes even big decisions can be changed. Teens and young adults may hesitate choosing because they think something better might come along. They do prefer exploring all their options, delaying as long as they can. They often doubt their own judgments, which makes it harder for them to mature.[12] They don't have to worry about trying to make the perfect, final decision. Change is possible. If they choose one college and discover that it's not a great fit, they can make a change after a semester or two. They can choose a different major from the one they thought they wanted on the first day of college.

3. We can provide guidance for the big decisions that aren't easily changed. There are some irreversible decisions! For example, the choice of a spouse is a lifetime commitment. We can help teens with this decision by talking through what traits they might look for in a life partner. We can suggest that they date only those who have the kind of traits they're looking for. Sometimes young people choose to leave behind their faith or choose a different religion. This is a big decision, and parents help the most by being engaged themselves in a local church, by talking openly about how God is shaping our lives through the Bible and our relationship with Him and with others, and by praying together as a family. And we can pray that the young people we love choose Christ as their Savior and never look back.[13]

But we can't be surprised that "the choice lie" creeps into the faith area of decision, too. After a presentation to a youth group, a teen told me he couldn't choose Jesus as his Savior even though it made sense because he might discover a better choice the next day. A youth pastor I know well relayed a similar incident. At the summer camp after a teen's senior year, this young man told Jeff that rather than trusting Christ he wanted to see what was offered at the college he'd be attending.

4. We can ask deep questions that make teens think. Rather than asking, "What are you going to do when you grow up?" and "Where are you going to college?" we could ask today's multi-talented, multipassionate teens a question like, "What problems would you like to help solve?" I've had some amazing conversations with youth that began with this question. In their answers we'll often see connections to high school electives, college majors, and careers, so it can stimulate a great conversation. Here's one of several Facebook messages I received from a mom who took my recommendation seriously:

> In one of your workshops you said we should not ask our children what they want to be when they grow up but instead ask them what problem they want to help solve. I haven't been able to shake that thought. Tonight, I was lying beside our twelve-year-old daughter for her special mom time, and I asked her that question. I was stunned. Stuff started pouring out of her. Things I hadn't even heard her say before! . . . I also asked our youth girls this question and had a great response with it as well.

> There's a difference between telling teens what to do and teaching them how to do it.

5. We can stay engaged with our teens. Teens will usually listen better to us if we've been talking with them their whole lives. It's not too late—ever—but we'll have to work harder to earn their trust if we haven't been directly and intimately involved in their comings and goings. Too many teens ask me what happened when they turned thirteen. They talk about how their parents' sudden interest seems like interference because they hadn't been very involved before. For example, "Yesterday they trusted me and didn't seem to care who I was with or why I was doing what I was doing. I had a birthday and now they care." Or, I hear things about becoming middle-schoolers. "I'm older and in a different school, and now my dad cares." Sometimes they add "But I don't care anymore." That's the risk. If we've been absent in any way, we need to apologize and not try to deny there's truth in their observations and concerns. We can admit we trusted them and thought they were safe when young, but we shouldn't have been as absent as they sense we were. We can ask them if they'll let us care. We will certainly care no matter how they respond, but the conversation may secretly mean a lot to them.

> **Often one** choice leads to another, which leads to another. This is a natural part of life.

6. We can teach our teens to choose well. There's a difference between telling them what to do and teaching them how to do it. Simply telling them what to do keeps them dependent upon us. We can't afford to only offer advice and opinion. That weakens our case. These are too easily dismissed, especially if our teens don't respect us. Our teens deserve more. We must instruct—impart knowledge, teach, and allow our children to obtain their own wisdom through application of what we have passed along. We must train—help them form habits and develop proficiency. Then we must carefully correct—adjust their behavior with action (not anger) so they'll follow the teaching and training.

Some parents will offer actual lessons about choosing well. Family devotions with a theme of decision-making is another way to teach. Other parents create opportunities to talk about how to choose. Others wait for opportunities to teach that present themselves in the everyday happenings of life. In addition to what we've already covered in this chapter, we can include:

- *Mindfulness.* Since many teens are quick, prefer instant gratification, and use their first impressions when choosing, we can teach how, why, and when a more careful and detailed analysis of the situation is warranted. Eric Metaxas is one of many recommending the practice of mindfulness: "Being mindful involves slowing down and doing things deliberately. It forces attention where we might otherwise merely act reflexively. Such practice builds the mind's capacity for self-control."[14]

- *Moral choices vs. wisdom choices.* Explain the difference between moral choices (a matter of right versus wrong) and wisdom choices (good versus better or best). Especially if our teens seem regularly satisfied with "good," observe to see if we can figure out why and help them to discover better or best.

- *Preferences vs. decisions.* We can talk about the differences between simple decisions, which are really preferences (such as eggs or cereal for breakfast, the blue or the red shirt), everyday decisions that become habits based on character (exercise five out of seven days, tell the truth, honor people's time), and major decisions that probably should involve thinking, feeling, intuition, and talks with trustworthy people in and beyond the family. Look for simple and everyday choices to get easier and then guide them so major choices also get easier.

- *Choices as a part of life.* Often one choice leads to another, which leads to another. This is a natural part of life. Teens who are hesitant to make a choice because it limits their choices benefit from understanding that they'll always be making choices. For example, even after choosing to follow Christ, there are decisions we continue to make—like being truthful, honoring our word, protecting our relationships, and others.[15]

THE TRUTH WE WANT TEENS TO BELIEVE

No one likes to watch our teens being tossed to and fro, torn in their emotions from indecision or feeling overwhelmed. When Jesus becomes the anchor for our teens, they'll have a refuge against the cultural tides (choices) that pull them in myriad directions. By standing firm in Him, they will have made the right choice and will thrive.

What's the truth we want our teens to believe instead of the lie that they must always have choices? The truth is: While I'm offered many choices, there are times it's appropriate for me to not have a choice. I'm grateful for all the options I often get, but that doesn't mean I'm incapable of handling it when I don't have any. When I do have options, I can learn to choose well, which includes considering what God would prefer me to do.

Lie #3: I must have choices.
Truth #3: I can handle my choices with God's help.

Trust in the Lord with all your heart
and lean not on your own understanding;
In all your ways submit to him,
and he will make your paths straight.

PROVERBS 3:5–6

7

LIE #4: I AM MY OWN AUTHORITY

By this time, you are not going to be surprised that today's young people have a difficult time understanding and appreciating authority. As teens in every generation separate from their parents, they tend to go through a phase of resisting or outright challenging authority. However, this generation doesn't just disregard authority, they think they can be their own authority.

The lies we've already covered play right into this one. Teens don't need to listen to anyone if they're the center of their own universe. They prefer doing their own thing since happiness is important to them. Making choices using the "universe" and "happiness" as criteria doesn't require teens to consider what someone older and wiser recommends. Many teens don't believe they need advice or direction. They believe they are their own authority.

Have you seen teens disrespect authority? See if these causes ring true.

EVIDENCE OF THE LIE:
REASONS WHY AND THINGS TO TRY

Parenting Style

There are three parenting styles that play into this authority lie: the Friend Parent, the Absent Parent, and the Inconsistent Parent.

Friend Parents are so devoted they almost worship their kids. They want to be their children's friends! They allow their teens to do what they want, believe they can do no wrong, and have a hard time saying no. These parents either don't bother teaching standards for right and wrong, or they do try to establish such standards but in confusing ways. These children don't experience much authority, if any, and this freedom communicates to them, *You don't need authority. You can do what you want.*

The children of Absent Parents draw the same conclusion but for different reasons. These parents just aren't there for their kids. They're too busy with work or with personal problems, or they can't be bothered. They force early independence upon their children and cause them to parent themselves. Essentially these teens become their own authority by default.

Inconsistent Parents might treat children like friends one minute, but not the next. They may be heavy-handed one day, but then lighten up as they feel guilty over the way they just responded to their children. Sometimes they may order their kids around and at other times be completely absent. These children have a warped view of authority and may think, *If that's what authority is and does, I don't need any.* In these situations, the children will be confused, drifting, and argumentative.

If, right about now, you're feeling tremendously insecure about your parenting mistakes (and every parent makes them!), take heart.

1. We can change! If you fall into one of these parenting categories and don't like it, change is possible. It will take effort and talking with your children to explain why you're making some changes. Have they been ignoring you? Resenting you? Talking back? Complaining? Apologize for your specific part in creating these problems, if you feel it's appropriate. You also may want to spend time with parents who use a style you want to adopt. You can observe how they make decisions and interact with their kids. Initially your children may resist you, but stay the course because it *will* be to the benefit of all.

2. We can resist the temptation to judge other parents. If you're confident in your parenting style and don't believe it negatively affects your children's opinions about authority, don't waste time judging other parents. Keep your eyes and ears open to parents who may want your help, and help as a peer if you are asked. With humility, be honest about your successes and lessons learned from your struggles. You might begin or help to promote a parenting class at your church. Parenting isn't easy today for many reasons, and a lack of healthy authority, or teens' respect for authority, are underlying causes.

Authority Failures

Let's admit there are plenty of reasons for young people to be skeptical. Just look around. We've had authority figures in every arena be accused of character flaws, faulty decisions, or inappropriate actions. Because of our instant media technology, we become aware of almost every detail. Government. Church. School. Nonprofits. Corporations. Media. Families. We've lost respect for authority because we've lost respect for authority figures. Teens may be slow to trust us or any exercise of authority with good reason.

All of us in positions of authority, and that includes all parents, need to guard our hearts and minds.

How can we influence our young people's view of authority figures, despite the failure all around them?

1. We can guard our hearts and minds. All of us in positions of authority, and that includes all parents, need to guard our hearts and minds. We can use accountability systems and allow select people in our lives to provide accountability. There are numerous proverbs that instruct us to seek godly counsel (such as Proverbs 12:15 and 15:22) and warn us against believing we know enough (Proverbs 11:14 and 13:10). When we make mistakes, morally compromise, or sin, we need to take personal responsibility, without ducking the consequences. We need to forgive ourselves and ask to be forgiven, as appropriate.

2. We can help teens process the failure of authority figures. When teens learn of people's failures, be available to help them process what happened and how they're feeling. These are great opportunities to model grace, mercy, and compassion even while we hold tight to biblical standards. Processing experiences well may help our teens trust authority figures again.

3. We can highlight wise authority figures. Though they may be few and far between, some authority figures do use their authority well and can be trusted with the authority they have been given. I sometimes tell young people about my grandfather on my mom's side. He was the mayor of my city when I was young, and he's one of my heroes. One Christmas Day when it began to snow, my brother, cousins, and I were thrilled. But I saw tears in my grandfather's eyes. He knew he'd have to ask snowplow drivers to leave their families to ensure the safety of our community. My grandfather knew these hardworking drivers would have to sacrifice important family and celebration time. Yet my grandfather shouldered that responsibility, knowing he'd been elected to take care of the whole community's welfare, even when a situation required a tough decision.

Television and Movies

Many reality and competition shows accentuate values contrary to those of most Christians, and many disregard authority.

Many popular productions have no authority figures in them at all, or the people in authority are not portrayed in a positive light. After asking for input on Facebook, one person said this about television shows: "Children talk back, and the parents are represented as pushovers, dumb, unaware, uninvolved, or stupid." I agree! I just heard a commercial advertising something simple end with this line: "Even a parent can do it."

Friends of mine have purchased DVD box sets of shows their children like to watch even though they're available as reruns on some channels. They don't want their children watching them on TV because authority is disrespected even in the commercials their daughters would see.

Here are other proactive ways we can lead our teens to respect and value authority in their lives.

1. We can be closely aware of what our kids are viewing. We need to be aware of what our teens are watching through various services and on their devices. It's not simple anymore—we need to work at this by keeping them accountable and keeping screen access in the family areas of the home.

2. We can explain the *why* behind good media choices. We can explain our standards for what we believe is and is not appropriate when our kids are young and adjust them as they mature. If they know *why* we believe what we believe, they might adopt our same beliefs even when we're not directly involved. Isn't that part of the goal of "training up children in the way they should go"? One family I know uses a Focus on the Family website, Plugged In.[1] When their kids were younger they would read movie reviews to determine what was appropriate for their kids to see. As their kids entered middle school and started asking to go to movies with friends, they would require their teens to read the movie review on Plugged In on their own to determine if the movie would be appropriate. Many times the teens would come to their own conclusions simply by reading the content reviews; sometimes they wouldn't even ask to go to a particular movie.

3. We can watch together. Watching shows and movies together and talking about characters, their motivation, plot development, language, and subtle messages can be one of the best ways to pass on our values. Some families have regular movie nights, which can also bond siblings. Going to movies one-on-one with children can be effective for talking about authority, culture, and more. Plan on dinner, dessert, or a walk after the movie to allow time to process and discuss what you just saw. Look for the ways authority is handled in the films you see. Who's wielding the power? How do others respond to those exercising authority? These talking points open a door for exploring the issue with your teen.

Other Technology

Much of today's gaming makes the gamer feel in complete control, which feeds the authority lie. All the decision-making associated with surfing the Web and scrolling on social media sites also feed into the computer user's feeling of being the master of his online universe.

Without discernment, it's hard for teens to know who or what to believe.

At the same time it's handing the user a feeling of freedom and control, the World Wide Web is . . . confusing. It's a wide, wild world of opinions and information (good and bad). There is, without doubt, a whole lot of lying going on. As someone posted on Facebook, "We live in a world where anybody can sit behind a keyboard and say whatever they want to virtually anybody with no real repercussions." So how does that opinion overload affect a young person's view of authority? Without discernment, it's hard for them to know who or what to believe. So they pick and choose, becoming—yep!—their own authority.

Texting, social media, and email offer teens a wide freedom to communicate, without any accountability to authority. There's no one to stop social media users from lying or disrespecting others; comments can be made without the intervention that would take place when people are talking face-to-face. Social media sites like Facebook make it easy to comment on everything, with strong appeal for teens who may not feel heard by others, narcissists who enjoy self-promotion, or bullies who disagree often with people's posts and comments. Some seem to derive a twisted kind of pleasure by undermining everything posted online. Also, some teens post their own or share other people's videos and photos that display people's weaknesses. It can be a vicious, dangerous world— and teens are on their own out there!

So what can parents do to take back some authority on these hard-to-monitor technology issues?

1. We can increase face-to-face time with our kids. Having designated zones and times for connecting are critical. The more we interact with our teens in real face-to-face times, the better. Don't expect this to be easy. Teens will resist. Stand firm for what you know they need even if they say they don't want the time with you.

2. We can monitor their social media interaction. We can help our children by regularly examining their social media posts, their comments there, and their comments on friends' posts. Especially when they're beginning to use these services, we can present ourselves as the authority they need because we *are* the authority they need. This will be especially important if they're being hassled in any way online. As discussed in the last chapter, we need to

> **The culture** at large may not have any consensus on what's right and wrong, but your family culture can provide that crucial moral compass for your teens.

teach them how to respect themselves and their friends and not just *tell* them what concerns us.

Lack of a Clear Standard

Having lost our cultural moral consensus makes it easier for teens to believe their own standard is as good as anyone else's. It's so easy for them to drift and second-guess the values they've been taught. Not having a clear compass for life makes rejecting authority easy. Teens may act according to moods or gut feelings, with the result of unwise, unfortunate decisions—some of them with lasting consequences.

The culture at large may not have any consensus on what's right and wrong, but your family culture can provide that crucial moral compass for your teens.

1. We can help teens see how God's authority is designed to protect them. God's boundaries come out of His love for us. Right and wrong are established to protect us from consequences that will hurt us. For instance, "Do not steal" protects us from losing the trust of others, and "Do not have sex before marriage" protects us from sexually transmitted diseases and being physically bonded to someone other than our spouse for life. In general, we need to see and present authority as a blessing to our teens. Specifically, we need to present the Word of God as the most trustworthy standard. It is reliable, consistent, and complete. We have freedom because He gives us free will, but that's also a reason He provides boundaries. Because God is merciful and full of grace, we can follow and fulfill His best for us with trust and without fear. This gets easier as we know and love Him more.

2. We can encourage teens to learn to hear God's voice. God speaks to us through the Holy Spirit, through the Bible, and through other believers. As we learn to hear God more clearly, we can share how we're learning to recognize His voice and what He is teaching us.

3. We can fully embrace a relationship with Jesus Christ ourselves. The more that God is in the driver's seat of our lives, the more influence we can have in encouraging our teens to let God lead theirs. Don't be discouraged if your teens initially reject a relationship with God. Continue loving them well and showing them in action what it looks like to trust God.

WHEN THEY RESIST THE ULTIMATE AUTHORITY

One of the greatest reasons to pay attention to how this "authority lie" affects our teens is that God may be the ultimate authority they reject. Because this is a matter of eternity, we must pay attention—really listen and watch—and speak up early if we're concerned. Nowhere is being aware of lies more important than when considering what our teens believe about God.

My prayer is that you believe as I do, that God is good (Mark 10:18) and God is love (1 John 4:8). We're grateful for His personal love, which motivates both our faith and our responses to His authority. We want—maybe desperately—for young people to know Him as we do.

However, our young generation's perspective about authority isn't healthy. That's one reason they are often less interested in God and the church. They see both as authority, yet there is so much more to God and His church!

Almost on a daily basis, you and I can read a new blog, email newsletter, or news report about the reality that many teens and young adults are disinterested in God.[2] They're leaving the church.

Some have faith and have appeared interested in Him in the past. Others have gone through the motions, perhaps to please their parents or because they felt they had no choice.

My staff and I pay attention to what's written, we observe young people, and we have talked at great length about teens' apparent confusion and apathy. We're convinced that many, if not most, don't have an accurate understanding of the holy and good God we love. Lies have confused them.

I need authority in my life, and I can learn to trust it.

In an effort to battle the authority lie and replace it with the truth that God's authority is safe for us, I've identified common beliefs (or lies) that too often drive young people away from God and His church. I've also identified the truths that combat the erroneous beliefs.

Take some time to study these truths and consider your own beliefs. Look up the verses from the Bible and solidify those truths in your heart. As you parent, begin to look for these lies that permeate our society. Speak truth whenever you can!

WHAT TO AVOID	WHAT TO MODEL AND TEACH
Believe just what I want to about Jesus.	See Jesus for who He truly is according to Scripture (Matt. 16:16; 1 Tim. 3:16; Heb. 1:3; Acts 4:12; John 20:31).
Believe what I want about God so pay attention only to certain ideas in the Bible, if I read it at all. I rely on my feelings about God.	Rely on what the Bible teaches about God. I know He doesn't change even if my feelings toward Him do. The whole counsel of God's Word contains absolute moral truth and is important to my life (2 Tim. 3:16; Heb. 4:12).
Participate in programs and systems. It's all about religion and ritual. It's the cost I must pay.	My personal relationship with God is established in faith, trust, and belief in Jesus, not in my good works (Rom. 5:10; Gal. 2:20; Eph. 2:6–10; Heb. 4:14–16).
Follow rules, working the tools.	Embrace Jesus in a dynamic relationship (Rom. 8:3; 10:10–11; Gal. 5:6).
Jesus is just one of many ways to heaven.	Trust Jesus because He died for my sin, rose from the dead, and is the only way to heaven (John 3:16–17; 1 John 4:15; John 14:6; Acts 4:12; Rev. 1:5).
Refuse to share anything about God because people have a right to their own beliefs.	Talking with others about God's truth and my faith in Jesus is a privilege and responsibility (Matt. 28:18–20; Mark 12:33; Acts 4:32–35).
Do the disciplines I feel I must do to stay in good standing with God or to get His attention. It's an effort.	Be grateful to God as Savior and, therefore, respond by reading, studying, and memorizing Scripture; praying; worshipping; serving; giving (2 Pet. 3:17–18; Eph. 3:17–20; 2 Tim. 3:16; Ps. 119:105).

Serve and work with excellence to earn my salvation and then keep it.	Serve with excellence to glorify God, edify others, and not simply for my own benefit. Everything necessary for my salvation was done by Jesus (Eph. 2:8, 9; 3:16–17; Rom. 9:16; 1 Thess. 1:3).
Plateau. Believe I have heard it all. Deny God after I've known Him.	Pursue God and grow in my faith because I have fallen in love with Him and want to (Eph. 4:22–24; Rom. 5:3–5).
God doesn't care about me.	Our heavenly Father is passionate for me and compassionate to me (Eph. 1:4; 18–19; Rom. 8:38–39; 1 Cor. 13).
I probably sin more and worse than others. That's all people seem to care about—my sin. That's probably all God cares about, too. He can't forgive my sin. I can't accept His forgiveness. My sin is too bad. I'm too bad.	Everyone sins. That's why Jesus came and died—to save everyone. Those in relationship with Christ, like me, have had all sin forgiven by God. Because of my relationship with Him, He sees me and not my sin (1 John 4:9; Ps. 130:2–4).
God holds present and future sins against us.	God's forgiveness and grace are real and complete. There is no shame or condemnation in Christ (Rom. 8:1–4; Rev. 1:5).
Take advantage of God's forgiveness. I can keep sinning because I've already been forgiven.	Be grateful for God's forgiveness, which I don't deserve. His love is the greatest deterrent from sin (Col. 1:13; Rom. 6:1–14).
God is a heavy-handed, joy-zapper judge who just wants to control me. He only cares about rules.	God's authority is good for me and my life. His love empowers a grace-filled manifestation of the fruit of the Spirit that results in freedom. Rules have no power to save me (Gal. 5:22–23; Eph. 5:15–21; Rev. 1:5).

God's ways are limiting.	Jesus came to set us free (Gal. 5:1; John 8:31–32).
God has designed a rigid structure with no individualization.	God has a good plan for me. He treats me as a unique individual and doesn't use a formula (Job 10:8–9; Jer. 29:11; Ps. 139).
Christianity emphasizes sin and brokenness.	God is full of grace and mercy (Heb. 4:16; Ps. 130:2–4).
God's love for me is conditional based on my choices. I love Him the same way—it's conditional.	God's love is unconditional (Jer. 29:11; John 3:16–17; Lam. 3:21–24; Rom. 8:39; Eph. 2:3–5).
Fear God and His wrath and, therefore, try to be good enough.	Love God and delight to honor Him with my choices (Deut. 6:5; Josh. 23:11; Micah 6:8; 1 John 4:16–21).
If I'm saved, it's about having fire insurance.	Enjoy a purposeful, joyful life now and know I will in eternity, too (Ps. 19:14; Col. 3:17; 1 Cor. 10:31; Eph. 5:15–21).
God and His Word are out of date and are irrelevant to me now.	God and His Word are the same yesterday, today, and tomorrow and remain relevant to me (Heb. 13:8; Ps. 12:6; 2 Tim. 3:16; Ps. 119:89; Eccl. 1:9).
Prayer is me asking for things I want and treating God like an answering machine. Get quickly disappointed or angry when I don't get what I want.	Prayer is a vibrant two-way relationship where I get to know God better and I am willingly transparent because He already knows me better than I know myself (Phil. 4:6; 1 Thess. 5:16–18; James 5:13; Ps. 119:62; Matt. 7:7; Eph. 1:15–17).

God doesn't meet my needs and is only concerned about my behavior.	God meets my core needs and cares about what I think and feel (Phil. 4.6; Matt. 6:25–39; Ps. 37:4).
God can't be trusted, but I can trust myself.	All things work together for good for those who love God (Rom. 8:28; Ps. 9:10; Ps. 13:5–6; John 14:1; Rom. 15:13).
I am self-sufficient.	God is sufficient. He is more than enough for me (Job 12:10; Ps. 31:3; Isa. 26:12; Prov. 16:9).
I lead; God is in agreement with what I want.	Allow and want God to lead; I follow well (Ps. 143:10; Prov. 18:2; Ps. 73:23; Isa. 41:13; Prov. 1:7).
God needs me to help Him figure out who the true Christians are.	God knows the bigger picture and is the only One who knows our hearts. Faith in Christ is personal and is lived out uniquely (Matt. 9:2; Luke 7:50; 2 Tim. 1:8–9; Jer. 29:11; Rom. 12:6).
I can be perfect so I don't need God.	Only God is perfect (Deut. 32:4, Ps. 14:2–3; Ps. 18:30; Isa. 6:1–3; Rom. 3:10–12; Rom. 3:23; 1 Sam. 2:3; Matt. 5:48).

THE TRUTH WE WANT TEENS TO BELIEVE

Given all that is going on in our culture, it's understandable that many teens believe the lie that they are their own authority. Talk with them about why they might believe it, why it's dangerous, and what it would take for them to change their minds.

You and your teens might arrive at a true statement to replace the lie. It might be something like this: *I am willing for my parents and selected others to have authority in my life. I know they're not perfect and they may disappoint me, but that doesn't mean I can't humble myself and follow them, not blindly, but wisely. I think trusting God will be helpful, and I will let my parents and pastors help me learn how to do that well. Submitting to trusted and wise authority in my life will benefit me and the people I most care about.*

Lie #4: I am my own authority.
Truth #4: I need authority in my life, and I can learn to trust it.

Have confidence in your leaders
and submit to their authority.
Hebrews 13:17

8

LIE #5: INFORMATION IS ALL I NEED SO I DON'T NEED TEACHERS

Technology can be our best friend, and technology can also be the biggest party pooper of our lives. It interrupts our own story, interrupts our ability to have a thought or a daydream, to imagine something wonderful, because we're too busy bridging the walk from the cafeteria back to the office on the cellphone.

STEVEN SPIELBERG[1]

Teens want information, especially that relevant to their personal interests and the problems they'd like to help solve, but young people may believe they don't need to go deeper and actually seek wisdom. Information satisfies them. Because many don't prioritize going deep, they don't believe they need teachers. As a result, many do not recognize their need for guidance. Some ignore us and some unfortunately may drop out of school and church. This is especially true if they believe that they are their own authority.

Stopping at information, short of seeking wisdom and guidance, short-circuits young people's progress toward future dreams and their worthy plans for changing the world. Frustration sets in as they discover they're not totally prepared to be the change agents they want to be. The "information lie" is a subtle one, and young people may not realize that information is not enough.

As we explore the causes for this "information lie," you may discover that some of them are particularly relevant for the teens you love. Beyond the suggestions I can offer, I pray your imagination will be sparked to develop strategies for positively influencing their attitudes toward you, teachers, and pastors. Ponder how you might inspire them to yearn to learn and become more teachable.

EVIDENCE OF THE LIE:
REASONS WHY AND THINGS TO TRY

Teens Are Intuitive with Technology

These days even young children can figure out how to work handheld devices. A Facebook friend posted that she was watching a show on Netflix when her two-year-old approached. He picked up the remote, found the show he wanted to watch, and started watching it. Her post ended with, "I guess I'm done watching my show. Lol."

That post didn't make me want to laugh out loud. Sure, this toddler's intuition with technology is obvious, but this was a perfect moment for teaching him that having strengths doesn't mean he automatically gets to use them. As an adult authority figure, she had every right to watch her program and redirect her son to something else. It was a perfect opportunity to teach him self-control and respect for authority. Her passive submission to his television takeover taught the young boy a different lesson: He doesn't need an authority or teacher.

So how can we help teens see that technology in itself is a tool, part of a much wider world of skills and competencies?

1. We can help them understand the limits of their technology intuition. Even while you affirm teens' skills and efficiency with technology tools, help them see that other problems can't be solved with equal intuitive ease. Show your teen when you're facing situations that call for a skill set beyond the technology. Maybe you're working out a tricky problem at work that requires complex reasoning ability and hanging on to many details or threads of information. Technology can help, but it can't solve the whole problem. Maybe a conflict within your church family is resolved with great wisdom and dependence on the application of peace, patience, and self-control among the people involved. Maybe a twenty-something person you know is carefully implementing a long-term plan toward a certain career or is achieving some sort of artistic or business success. Your adult perspective can help make your teen aware of the reasoning skills, character development, reaching out for advice, and dependence on God's guidance involved in these projects.

Intuitive technology skills are wonderful, but they don't automatically lead to success in academics, problem-solving, interpersonal relationship–building, and future planning. As you name, articulate, and explain other goals for gaining maturity, young people may begin to move their view of technology from an end or purpose in itself to a tool that joins many others in equipping them for adult life.

2. We can familiarize ourselves with technology as much as possible. It's fine, of course, for you to turn to your teens for help with your technology. Their talent and intuition with technology are a gift to your family. But I recommend that you not depend solely on your kids' help with technology, but learn what you can. And handle it with care when you do ask them for help. Of course we want them to know we value what they have to offer and we are learners, but we also want teens to retain their respect for us as authority figures. It can be confusing to kids when we're their authority or teacher one moment and their student the next.

Teens Long to Be Self-Sufficient

Today's young people can be very independent. The Internet is partly responsible because it so strongly affirms the cultural rite of independence and equates it to personal control and freedom. Teens can also learn a lot on their own because of wonderful games and apps they use for learning

> **Some measures** of independence are part of growing to adulthood.

and memorizing basic facts.

It's become a norm for children and teens to need only a very short time span between learning about a

Embracing the wisdom of others doesn't mean we have to become dependent on them.

new game and playing it or a new song and listening to it. Because they don't need help with technology, they often transfer this independence to other areas.

Obviously, some measures of independence are part of growing to adulthood. Teens know we're getting them ready to manage school and work schedules without our input, pay for their own car and its insurance, handle their own apartment lease, and manage adult relationships well. Even though more self-sufficiency is the goal, we don't want to give young people the impression that adults don't need the wisdom and influence of authorities in our lives. So how can we help?

1. We can explain and model that allowing others to influence and teach us is a mark of maturity. We can help teens understand that embracing the wisdom of others doesn't mean we have to become dependent on them. We don't use advisors or teachers *instead of* learning on our own. We do both. You can model this in your relationships, as your young people watch you interact in a marriage, a business partnership, or other friendships. You model this by becoming part of a local church family, where your membership means you agree to submit to church authorities and to submit to one another within that community.

Wise adults are learning all the time. It's a mark of adulthood.

2. We can help teens see how we choose outside influences. Talk about how you chose a college or career, how you've chosen personal mentors, how you came to choose certain people (living or dead) as heroes. Tell teens about how doctrine and teaching influenced your choice of a local church family. Talk about what kinds of teaching styles appeal to you—personal, inspiring, storytelling, factual and detailed, whatever. Teens will already have encountered teachers and other adults who have influenced them. Help them analyze what made those particular people so influential. As you help them articulate what they value in teachers and mentors, you give them tools for choosing influences in the future. Teens have a lot of voices speaking into their lives, and it's a tough challenge to choose the wisest, best influences. They need adult help in shaping those discernment skills.

3. We can be humble and teachable ourselves. Our own ability to accept correction and instruction and the influence of others gives us the right to talk with our kids about these qualities. We can explain that others often help us see our blind spots. Others simply have experienced more than we have, and they can help us grow more than we can grow on our own. We were created to be strong, self-confident image-bearers of God while at the same time He designed us for healthy interdependency with each other. There are simply some things we cannot, and should not, do on our own. We are better as individuals when we have mutually benefitting relationships within our community. Ecclesiastes says, "two are better than one" and "a cord of three strands is not quickly broken" (4:9–12). Model this kind of teachable teamwork for your young people.

4. We can point teens to the ultimate example, Jesus. If our teens know Christ or are open to Him, we can remind them that even Jesus learned at the feet of others when He was young (Luke 2:46–52) and constantly listened to the Father and told His disciples what the Father said. Jesus' years of ministry were shaped by the teacher-plus-disciples model. He came to teach. Jesus was called "Teacher" more often than any other name,[2] and those who became His followers stayed open to learn from the Master. Scripture has many passages about learning and teaching that you might explore as a family.[3]

Teens Are Easily Turned Off by Outdated Materials and Slow-Paced Teaching

Considering the other lies we've discussed, together with the fact that the entertainment culture has crept into every area of teens' lives, it shouldn't surprise us that children reject many of their textbooks as outdated. Also, in their words, "talking-head teachers" are inefficient and too slow for their quick-paced, multitasking minds. They're so used to obtaining speedy answers on their digital devices, they'd rather not discipline or apply their minds.

Young people can miss a lot by dismissing what they believe is outdated. How can we help them accept the authority of older people, older works, and older or slower communication methods?

1. We can explain the values behind our own choices. If you're reading a classic book or watching a film series without fast pacing or computer-graphic imaging, take a few minutes to explain your own choice. What's valuable in those books and films that keeps you going back to them? If you're handing your children obviously dated material, direct them to its value as you hand it over, helping to motivate them even before they begin to read. Many parents are surprised to discover their young people developing an enthusiasm for the writing and thinking of previous generations. It gives parents and teens a great point of connection as they talk about what a work meant to different generations of readers.

The "drawing room" novels of Jane Austen are two hundred years old, but teen and twenty-something readers and moviewatchers gravitate in droves to the books and to remakes of these stories—either period pieces or modern versions of the stories (even YouTube dramatizations!). What draws contemporary women to stories from such an era of personal and sexual restraint? The personalities of Austen's characters are, well, timeless. How wonderful that this generation of young people isn't missing out on those great stories.

My friend Annette has consistently handed her teens the works of Francis Schaeffer and A. W. Tozer and J. I. Packer, theologians whose writing sparked recent generations of young thinkers—and her teens have loved these works and gone on to explore more by these authors. Consider the ongoing best-seller-status of books by C. S. Lewis, whose popularity with this generation remains un-diminished. Your teens have a wonderful opportunity to reach out for teaching from many generations.

Complaining just for the sake of complaining isn't healthy or productive, but looking for solutions is.

As they see you valuing "dated" materials and hear you talking about what you read and see, your teens may begin to wonder what they might be missing!

2. We can hear them out. If our children complain about materials and methods being used in school or church, we can listen for what we agree with and what we disagree with. Empathize if and when you can. If we believe helping our teens talk with teachers, pastors, and other authorities is appropriate and may help them make changes, we can do this. Our children will appreciate our support. If we believe our kids are wrong in their critique, we can discuss their opinions with them. We want to be open so our kids will talk with us. Shaping those conversations is critical, though. Complaining just for the sake of complaining isn't healthy or productive, but looking for solutions is.

3. We can give them skills for tackling what isn't easy. This impatient generation needs coping skills for learning perseverance and patience. Sometimes a book starts with a long, slow wind-up before it gets to the interesting pitch. Sometimes the language of an older work requires a teen repeatedly to tap into Merriam-Webster.com from his or her phone. As you help young people break big or hard tasks down into manageable parts or make yourself available to discuss difficult ideas, you help them conquer that "outdated, slow-paced" but worth-the-effort material. The successful endeavor will strengthen their own competence.

Teens Know Information Is Easy to Find

Websites, search engines, Siri, apps, videos, television documentaries, friends on social media, and other resources exist to help us efficiently get answers to our questions and information we seek. Today's children are missing opportunities to use higher thinking skills, when all they have to do is ask a phone a question or "Google" it.

So how can we help teens value information that takes more time and effort to obtain?

1. We can acknowledge the value of teens' ability to access information. Teens can quickly find information. That's a definite strength and value. We can encourage them to help us when we have a need to gather information for something.

2. We can help them value what they can get by digging deeper. While finding quick information is a strength, we need to encourage them to put forth effort to dig deeper than the first hit that comes up after a website search. We can model curiosity and talk about what we learned while spending more time exploring websites, using books, and comparing information across services.

3. We can help teens discern levels of reliability in information sources. Especially for those who often use websites for gathering information, we can search with them about a topic that interests them. As we open and peruse four to six resources, we discover that some sites offer shallow summations of a topic, some are incomplete, some are biased, and some contain contradictory information. Our input can help them develop skills for discerning reliable sources.

Teens can quickly accumulate lots of information on many topics and be distracted from actually landing on solid information leading to well-informed decisions and understanding.

This can compel them to seek more information when doing research in the future.[4]

Teens Enjoy Infotainment

Information satisfies teens. Because of the one-click-of-a-mouse search-engine mentality of our youth, many are satisfied with the information they find online. My friend Sy Rogers refers to this as "infotainment." Mere information is like eating donuts to satisfy us for the moment instead of taking in a full meal to nourish us for a longer time. Teens can quickly accumulate lots of information on many topics and be distracted from actually landing on solid information leading to well-informed decisions and understanding. "Everything matters, so nothing does."[5] Because young people think this quick search-and-grab is all they need, the role of "teacher" is unimportant.

> **Wisdom is** applying the right information in the right way in a relevant situation.

How can we help our young people reach out for more than just what entertains them?

1. We can be alert for teachable moments. Rather than waiting for teens to ask for help to go beyond information, which will often be hard for them to do, we can offer insights as we engage them in conversations. Talking together makes it easier to help them discover why simply being "infotained" is only satisfying in the moment; true knowledge and wisdom are more interesting, valuable, and life-giving.

2. We can help teens distinguish between knowledge and wisdom. We can explain the difference between information, knowledge, and wisdom. Information is data gathered; it may or may not be relevant or true. Knowledge is understanding a body of facts and the ideas inferred by those facts.[6] Wisdom is applying the right information in the right way in a relevant situation. "From a worldly perspective, knowledge helps you make a living, but wisdom makes a life."[7]

While we're mentioning wisdom, let's remember that Christian parents will want to narrow a general definition of *wisdom* to a godly view of wisdom. One writer defines spiritual wisdom as "the ability to apply the Word of God accurately and correctly, not only in the believer's life, but in the lives of others."[8] Affirm your teens when you see them applying God's wisdom—our Creator's good intent and guidance for our lives.[9]

Teens Are Comfortable with Perplexity

Teens can handle perplexity. More than the rest of us, this younger generation is comfortable not rushing to find answers. In their book *What a New Generation Really Thinks about Christianity . . . And Why It Matters,* David Kinnaman and Gabe Lyons conclude that young people "relish mystery, uncertainty, ambiguity. They are not bothered by contradictions."[10] Today's young people are willing to withhold judgment and may eventually draw conclusions on their own. They don't see the need for a teacher to help them in many important areas of life because they'll use their own opinions.

It's great that teens can handle perplexity and contradictions; most adults realize they must live with a great many mysteries. But a teen's comfort with uncertainty and ambiguity becomes a disadvantage when it keeps him or her from pursuing truth or from grappling with big issues. Teens need adults to offer wisdom and teach discernment skills and model perseverance so that they don't get so comfortable with perplexities that they stop working toward the truth. How can we help?

1. We can acknowledge ambiguities. It's healthy to admit complexities that are real. When teens do ask questions, it's better if we avoid overly simplistic answers or suggestions for their problems. They can handle some complexity! It's also best to humbly admit when we can't explain something.[11] Many of us may get stressed when not able to reconcile ideas. Or we may rush to conclusions because we don't like ambiguity. Being able to handle perplexity can be a good thing, but teens need to see trusted adults handling ambiguities in a healthy manner.

2. We can share about times in our lives when we, too, held conflicting ideas. We can share what sometimes caused us to arrive at solid conclusions and why we're glad we did. We can assure teens that wrestling with truth is okay—it's a good thing to do! Knowing we have this shared experience may encourage teens to talk with us when they want to draw firm conclusions about things.

3. We can help them agree to disagree with friends. Many teens are stressed about drawing conclusions because they don't want to alienate anyone who may draw a different conclusion. They're trying to keep their friends happy! They need adult input to help them discern when keeping friends happy is less important than endorsing what's true. We can guide them to the interpersonal skills they need to talk through disagreements with their friends and about how to handle friends who get upset because they disagree. Agreeing to disagree is an important skill for life!

4. We can embrace paradox in our faith journey. Since today's teens and young adults like mystery and the existence of complexities, discuss what a paradox means and create a fun exercise by asking them how many paradoxical ideas, or mysteries, they can find in Christianity. For example, this could include how both genders represent our Heavenly Father equally, how serving others and not focusing on ourselves usually turns out to bless us greatly, how God is both gentle and powerful, and how in losing our life we find it. Be ready for everyone to grow in understanding and faith!

> **Quiet and rest** benefit our thinking as attention, focus, and deep thinking are developed during quiet times.

Teens Are Rarely Quiet

Quiet and solitude are rare. Scientists know that our brains benefit from rest,[12] and our own experiences bear out this truth. Quiet and rest benefit our thinking as attention, focus, and deep thinking are developed during these times.[13] Chapman and Pellicane concluded, "The constant noise of the Internet, media, and video games is a huge barrier to creative thought and the development of deep thinking in children."[14]

When writing for the *New York Times* about the tendency to reach for devices when bored, Sherry Turkle concludes, "Reaching for a device becomes so natural that we start to forget that there is a reason, a good reason, to sit still with our thoughts: It does honor to what we are thinking about. It does honor to ourselves."[15]

Solitude allows teens to refine their own ideas. Silence increases the likelihood teens will hear God's voice. Both of these encourage meditation. Times of focused reflection on God's Word, His truths, and other things teens value and want to get clear about help them choose wisdom over information. Often this helps young people realize they need teachers.

How can we help them practice quietness?

1. We can increase the quiet in our homes. Instituting face-to-face connecting zones and media-free days will increase quiet in our homes. Encouraging everyone in the family to spend some of these times alone will help our kids learn to value both solitude and quiet.

2. We can let our kids see us spending time with God. Having our devotions in a place where our kids can see us, at least occasionally, is a great way to model spending time alone with God because of our love for Him. We can talk about what we gain from these times. When we share, we need to present it for what it is—something normal and expected when spending time with God. If we amp up the spiritual language and make a big deal out of everything, we can intimidate our teens. They may think they're not as spiritual if they don't have elaborate spiritual experiences all the time. Our relationship and times spent with God are special, but we do not have to glow like Moses or make some big show of hearing from Him every time we do.

HELP THEM GET COMFORTABLE
WITH ACCEPTING TEACHING

Parents can help their teens in two big-picture ways. The first is to be the leader/teacher, and the second is to help teens organize and consider the information coming at them.

Guide and Lead Them

Because teens have never known life without technology and its wonderful advantages, they prefer to investigate and discover truth on their own. We can think in terms of them constructing ideas rather than us instructing them in ideas. We facilitate learning rather than transmit ideas. Many teens will resent us if we present ourselves as experts and treat them as blank slates.

And we are wise to find out what they know. Not only will this help our teaching, they'll also see we value them and their experiences. This enhances our relationship. But they need our wisdom and strength to guide and lead them to reject the extraneous and the false and to learn more about what's relevant and true. We can think of them as researchers who investigate ideas and reporters who complete assignments. They learn to verify and re-verify before believing and reporting. [16]

Teach Them How to Sift, Sort, Synthesize, and Share[17]

Because many teens have been satisfied with information, thinking skills and study strategies may not be areas of strength. Also, because of the other lies they believe, these skills don't come naturally to them. For example, they want things to be easy and they want to keep people happy. So by modeling and working alongside them, we can teach teens to sift and sort, synthesize, and share.

Sift and sort. Teens need to learn how to sift and sort through all the information they have. The first sifting will usually be for what's true and what's false. Then the information that's true needs to be sorted into relevant categories depending on the goals. This can include things like relevant/irrelevant, important/unimportant, valuable only to me/valuable to others, complete /incomplete, healthy/unhealthy, right/wrong, and good for me/ bad for me.

> **Teens compartmentalize** bits of information more than they synthesize them into a meaningful whole.

Synthesize. I've been told by many educators and pastors that teens compartmentalize bits of information more than they synthesize them into a meaningful whole. They often keep information gathered from a variety of sources as separate. We can help them use ideas from one source to influence their interpretation of other ideas. Help them see connections between concepts, or how one piece of information applies to another.

Share. Because many teens are self-centered, they may need guidance in how to appropriately pass the information, knowledge, and wisdom on to others. They'll need to do this if they're going to improve the world by helping to solve problems. For example, we can find out if they'd like help with writing skills, public speaking, creating murals and dioramas, communicating through song, and the like. This can include specifics like learning to finish assignments and create products when purposes are different and with certain audiences in mind. For instance, are they writing to persuade or just to inform? Do they want their artistic interpretation to provoke thought or emotion or both? Do they want their song to simply entertain or inspire?

THE TRUTH WE WANT TEENS TO BELIEVE

Believing even just one of the lies that technology teaches our youth gives them an unhealthy view of themselves and the world. When believed collectively, these lies can especially confuse their beliefs and behaviors. For example, let's just consider how all the other lies affect this one about not needing teachers but only information.

- Teens who believe they're the center of their own universe want information that is relevant to them. They don't want teachers because teachers probably won't treat them as if the world revolves around them.
- Teens buying into the happiness lie feel that for them to stay happy, information has to be easy to find and understand. They're happier without teachers who could make them work hard to learn what they don't even value.

- Believing they must have choices is supported by all the information available on the Web and other technology. They may have a challenging time limiting their search and being satisfied.
- Their belief that they can be their own authority undermines the role of teachers. As their own authorities, they can teach themselves what they need to know.

Accepting the wisdom and instruction of others will bless and benefit young people throughout their whole lives—not just today in their schooling years, but also in their adult relationships in the family, in the workplace, and in church life. The truth we need teens to understand is, *I benefit from teachers helping me sift and sort through all the information available to me. Doing this well and then synthesizing what remains will help me arrive at knowledge and wisdom. When I realize these allow me to solve problems better than just information does, I'll value them and be willing to work on my own to more consistently prioritize them.*

Lie #5: Information is all I need so I don't need teachers.
Truth #5: I have much to learn from God and others and must seek wisdom above information.

Let the wise hear and increase in learning,
and the one who understands obtain guidance.
Proverbs 1:5 esv

9

THE ULTIMATE CONNECTIVITY

Connectivity has taken on new meanings in our age of digital tools. We need to be hooked up to the Web, linked in with colleagues, and interfacing with other computers. We're uploading and downloading and storing information in a Cloud! It's a whole new world of connectivity.

Being connected through our technology may make sense, but the human heart will always long for the deeper connection of person-to-person. The subtitle of this book is "Connecting with Our Kids in a Wireless World." *Connecting* may have been the word that caught your attention. Everywhere I go I meet parents

Whether it's in the family, church, school, or community at large, we reflect God's unity when connecting peacefully and intimately.

and grandparents, aunts, uncles, older siblings, teachers, church volunteers, and pastors who want to connect more often and more deeply with their children and grandchildren. I'm always grateful they haven't given up! I keep on praying that their connections will improve and grow. Living well together is beautiful. Whether it's in the family, church, school, or community at large, we reflect God's unity when connecting peacefully and intimately. That ultimate connectivity is so worth working toward!

Someone posted a photo of people waiting in a store line. Every single person in the line was intently focused on a cellphone in his or her hand. Teens walking to and from the local high school seem to move slowly and, often, alone. They they too are looking down at a cellphone in their hands. Screens are mesmerizing! It's hard to pull our eyes off them to register what's going on around us to or make eye contact with the living, breathing people near at hand.

A seven-year-old girl talks about wanting her parents' attention: "A lot of time when my parents are home and on their computers, I feel like I'm not here, because they pretend like I'm not there ... they're like not even talking to me, they just are ignoring me. I feel like, ughhh, sad [sigh]."[1]

Parents and young people can make adjustments in personal behaviors and family patterns that will promote a higher probability of connecting meaningfully. That deep connection will enable us to pass on our values and Christian worldview, talk openly about God and our faith journey, bring up character concerns, and talk about the value of teachers, wisdom, and authority.

When people understand the *why* behind what's driving beliefs and behaviors, change is more likely and more lasting. Maybe you and your kids are already connecting more often and in more satisfying ways. If so, good for you!

> **Although technology** can make connecting challenging, it's also true that online interactions *can* strengthen offline conversations.

Two more areas of focus can help promote this ultimate connectivity—conversations and contracts.

CONNECTIVITY THROUGH CONVERSATIONS

Children of all ages tell me they want and need to connect with their parents. They want to know *and* feel that parents care about them, their friends, and their activities. Having easygoing and meaningful conversations is an important way to do this. It takes skill and will—ability and strong desire.

Although technology can make connecting challenging, it's also true that online interactions *can* strengthen offline conversations. This is especially true if our relationships are already healthy. Connecting with our teens through social media, texting, FaceTime, and email positively affects teens' views of themselves and our face-to-face interactions.[2] Being present in your teens' online world is much more than being their "friend" and knowing their passwords so you can check up on them. It's about wanting to connect. Gaming with them might also deepen connections because you're joining them in something they enjoy doing.[3]

But the art of conversation can't be lost even if teens link sending a text message with "talking" to someone. In today's digital world we can't take for granted that our kids will learn actual conversation skills. It's going to take some intentional parenting to pass along the art of conversations. As you make an effort to improve conversation between you and your young people, here are some good guiding truths.

Interrogations Are Not the Same as Conversations

Sometimes teens tell me they can almost feel handcuffs tightening as they sit at the table and questions quickly follow one after another. They describe their parents' suspicious looks as being like a bright light focused on their eyes. They swear they're actually sweating as the heat and pace of the questions intensify. With great frustration, they proclaim, "Dr. Kathy, they treat me like I'm a suspect in a crime all the time!!"

Would your teens describe your interaction with them like this—more like the third degree than amicable discussion? Please note that I didn't ask if you'd describe your conversation this way, but if your teens would. It's their perception that matters. Interrogations won't help us connect, and getting grilled is one reason teens avoid interacting with their parents. There may be a time and a place for "not letting them off the hook," but most of us probably overuse this technique.

How do you get your teen's attention? Do you usually start with questions? Starting with a question can make your kids' interrogation radar come up—and the barriers to communication come down.

Questions are totally appropriate and necessary, but we can ask them so they don't feel like drive-by shootings or obligations to check off a list. If we want more in-depth honest answers, our questions and the way we ask them need to be fresh and genuine. How do our teens decide if that's the case? When we're really listening! When we connect and respond to their answers, when we try to feel what they're feeling, when we try to share in their experiences, when we to want to genuinely understand, and when our offers to help them are appropriate.

> **On the two-way** street of conversation, we can avoid head-on collisions and pay close attention if someone makes a U-turn.

Our questions can't be accusations hiding behind question marks. If you have a habit of continually bringing up past failures or offenses, kids may fear interacting with you because of what might be about to come up *again*. After an offense, teens do need to rebuild trust with their parents, but when something has been forgiven it needs to be relegated to the past and not constantly revisited. Let's make sure to model healthy forgiveness and reconciliation.

You might want to evaluate your interactions with your teens to see if they truly are two-way streets, with you talking and listening and your teens talking and listening. On the two-way street of conversation, we can avoid head-on collisions and pay close attention if someone makes a U-turn. Use active talking and listening, statements and questions, compliments and corrections, and laughter and serious reflection. We must model when and how to agree to disagree and when and how to push in and persuade. We must also model humility when we are incorrect in our observations and assumptions. Let's pay attention to and provide helpful feedback about eye contact, facial expressions, and body language so it matches our words and theirs.

If you've never developed a good conversational pattern with your teens, or if it's degenerated in recent months, this rhythm may not be easy to establish or reestablish. But don't give up. Try, try again. Our teens are too important not to!

Consider the Time and Place

When we were growing up, our dinner table was where my brother, Dave, and I knew we'd get to connect with each other and with our parents. Dave and I answered questions about our day. We knew our parents asked not just to check up on us, but because they cared. We knew because our parents were actively involved in our lives and didn't *need* to ask. They *wanted* to ask. These conversations were a natural part of living as a family. Gary Chapman and Arlene Pellicane write about protecting that family time over a meal: "Don't use the dinner table to preach or discuss stressful topics. Do that away from the table. At its best, dinner is about sharing stories, solving problems, no pressure, no meanness, no putdowns, no sarcasm—and no tech distractions."[4]

Decreasing the use of technology by implementing the connecting zones and connecting days we've discussed will create time and space for talking. Take advantage of it. Sometimes, as I described there, quiet is a great use of these times. So is play. But, talk, listen, listen, listen, talk.[5]

Talking in the car can work well because teens know we can't make much or any eye contact with them. This makes it easier to share challenging news. Teens will tell me, "Dr. Kathy, when I know I'm going to disappoint my parents, I don't want to see the hurt in their eyes. So the car is great. It's a great place to talk because they can't leave. They have to listen. Of course, so do I, because I can't run away either, but that's okay if they've listened to me."

Bedtime is another time and place teens prefer to talk. Even though we want our kids to get enough sleep and there's work we could do, some nights it pays to linger longer if they're in a talking mood. Just respond with, "And?" Or even plainly say softly, "Tell me more." We don't have to ask questions to get more information. Sometimes we just need to give them the space to talk without inserting our voice or our thoughts. Questions formed from restatements of relevant information they shared can indicate that we've listened, but our teens can quickly perceive when a free conversation they wanted to have turns into a judgmental interrogation we want to have.

Connect to Meet Deep Needs

We must step up and try again even if our teens seem rarely in the mood to talk with us or listen to us. For us to maintain our authority and influence in their lives, our teens must want to be connected to us and our relationship must be healthy. Once connecting through conversations is part of our shared expectations, talking will involve less effort and stress. If it seems you are unable ever to have a healthy conversation, you may want to seek family counseling. This can help bring buried issues to the surface so you can heal from the past and successfully move toward the future. Conversation can be restored!

At the very beginning of this book, we identified five core needs that must be met in healthy ways. Through listening and talking, we and our teens can be more *secure* in each other and ourselves. We can discuss character qualities and provide information to increase kids' confidence. Simply pursuing them because we want to connect through conversations increases our teens' security and confidence. Don't expect to hear "thank you." The exact opposite might occur at first. Pursue anyway.

Our *identity* can become more complete, accurate, and positive as we share. Our teens want to be known and they want to talk about themselves with someone who understands them or who wants to. We must be these significant, influential people. What a privilege!

Conversation will remind us that we *belong* to each other, and we'll understand better why we're connected. We'll discover our teens really do want to connect even if they haven't expressed it well lately. During conversations we can discover or remember common interests, hobbies, and family traits, while we bond over them.

As we talk, our *purpose* as parents, teens, and our particular family can become clearer for today and tomorrow. We'll see how it springs from our security, identity, and belonging and supports all three. Families share many purposes. Sometimes I think my family members—spread now across different states—believe we exist to support the Green Bay Packers. We are Packer Backers without apology! On game days we wear Packer shirts and green and gold beads and cheese-head earrings. We use cheese-head coasters and eat our tailgate-style food on Packer plates. Every Christmas, at least one person will get new Packer socks as a gift. From our distant cities, we text furiously back and forth during games. We bond and connect over Packers football. Of course, that's not the only purpose we share. Christian families share the ultimate purpose that their love and service to one another will glorify God.

As we each share our needs and listen well, our *competence* will increase. We'll encourage teens to rely on certain qualities they have within and we'll help them identify people who can fill in the gaps. As teens become more secure in our relationship, through these healthy connections, they'll more often turn to us to help them solve problems and make decisions. That's connection.

Connecting through conversations also allows us to have faith-based discussions. The earlier our children turn to God to meet their needs for security, identity, belonging, purpose, and competence, the better. Of course, we can't force children to accept Christ or it wouldn't be a loving and trusted personal relationship with Him. That said, don't ever give up or stop praying about their relationship with God!

> **We want** our teens to adopt and live out a Christian worldview that puts God at the center of the universe.

A vibrant relationship with Christ is more than something that sustains us during challenges. That's why ongoing conversations are important. We want our teens to adopt and live out a Christian worldview that puts God at the center of the universe. Rather than making self-centered decisions, we want them to filter everything through what they know about God. Trusting Christ isn't just about being in heaven the day we die. It's about living for and with Him. Conversations help us teach and model this agenda for living.

We can emphasize the truths we've learned ourselves during conversations. Talking about how practically to apply what God is teaching us can be extremely relevant conversations (and even enjoyable!). This can strengthen teens' relationship with God and their ability to use the truths they know throughout the day. We can also use teachable moments and when the time is right, we can discuss sermons, current events, school assignments, and other issues they're thinking about.

The goal? Deep, meaningful, safe conversations.

CONNECTIVITY AND CONTRACTS

Contracts between a parent and a teen can cause a disconnect—the very thing nobody wants. Contracts often close down communication rather than invite it. Many contracts are demeaning to one party or both. They can communicate that we don't trust our children to think things through and make wise choices. They don't take into consideration that life gets in the way of living! For example, our teens can't control what they'll be doing when their phone rings or which music might be played at a party. They can't guarantee a friend will choose a movie we'd approve of to watch when having friends over. To expect them to control any of this, bring it up to their peers, and report back to us is unrealistic and stressful.

You may have responded in your mind, *But I **don't** trust my kids!* Please know a contract might make you feel better, but by itself it won't build trust. It can communicate "I don't trust you, therefore you will sign this." It can actually build deceit and mistrust as kids violate something in the contract, but don't tell you. They may learn to hide or to lie. They may judge you harshly as they observe you violating the very principles you say are in their best interest. Most will do this silently or with siblings. They'll learn not to trust you.

What connects with kids? What builds their trust? Honest, detailed communication about what our expectations are and what we'll do and why if they disregard them. This is where contracts may help—when you lay down initial guidelines and family expectations.[6]

Our consistent life of love for them must compel us to instruct and guide— and not just talk.

Start talking about technology and tech issues as early as you can—when kids are young, if that's possible. Our consistent life of love for them must compel us to instruct and guide— and not just talk. We're in the business of passing on our God-honoring worldview, and this will take healthy connections based on growing relationships and regular conversations.

Rather than laying down a lecture, we need to have conversations that communicate our optimism and include relevant instruction. We need to be in the right mood and not rushed so we can share together while going for a walk, sitting in their bedrooms, and doing things we all enjoy. Remember, we want to avoid the handcuffs and bright, white light effects. We shouldn't be afraid of their ideas and questions, but openly discuss them and incorporate what we can. Shared power gives us more unity, strength, and influence.

If you've been using a contract, I hope you're becoming empowered to move your teens toward the day when they can make wise decisions when there's no contract in place. Discuss with your teens about growing into a stage when they can make wise decisions for themselves without a contract to do the thinking for them.

Remember the five lies? For a contract to work, teens have to be willing to . . .

- be taught by someone other than themselves,
- view us as authority,
- let us limit and control their choices,
- not always prioritize personal happiness, and
- care about others.

Hello, challenge! Those are all the areas that are most difficult for teens! Rather than a contract that tells them what to do and what not to do, let's teach them what's best. If we parent them so they discover the lies they've believed are actually lies, they'll begin to long for the truth. We're in a position to connect and communicate so that truths become truer and truer as our teens embrace life.

They need to be taught how to *think* about technology. We do this through modeling and conversations rich with truth. We keep on guiding and leading, complimenting and correcting, listening and watching with a heart to understand. We keep on noticing what's right and not just what's wrong. We keep on implementing positive and negative consequences. More than anything, we keep on being present—parenting and learning with them, while knowing that's a sign of strength, not weakness. We keep on teaching, explaining, being open to their ideas, and answering their questions.

If you've been using a contract to guide your kids' tech time and tech decisions, work toward guiding your child to making those good decisions on their own. Approach changes not through the "letter of the law" but through the teaching opportunities afforded through relational grace.

At Celebrate Kids, we believe children are capable of age-appropriate wisdom when it comes to technology. So are adults! Guidance, teaching, and right character are certainly going to make wisdom more likely. And wisdom means applying the right information in the right way in a relevant situation. Using the Word of God accurately and wisely is part of the "right information" and the "right way."

To facilitate right thinking without the use of contracts, I recommend asking questions well. As you evaluate your own tech use and guide your family, don't hesitate to implement your own ideas and parameters based on what you've experienced and what will work for you and your family. You won't need all the questions I'm providing in this chapter. Trust your own judgment. Tweak the wording to sound like you. Work through these questions a few at a time, when your kids are old enough to engage with them. Begin with the questions you think will actually help your teens the most.

These questions are also available at ScreensAndTeens.com,

so that you can print them out for easier use. These are not contracts but simply conversation starters designed to engage teens and guide their thinking and not designed to control their behavior.

As you spend time in Q&A with your teens, continually assess whether your conversation reflects biblical values and a Christian worldview. Let that guide you toward places where change might be needed.

Thinking with Four Cs

Contact. What kind of online world do I want to have? Do I want it to be made up of more people than just those who make me happy? Is this person who wants to connect with me (or who I want to connect with) someone I should allow into my online world? Would I want this person in my offline world? Would I want my parents to know we're connected?

Connect. Are my tech habits driving me away from my parents? Siblings? Others? Or are they helping me connect? Is anything I'm participating in negatively affecting my views of authority?

Conduct. Is my behavior appropriate? Am I being the "me" I know I want to be? Does this tech or social network help me with my growth and maturity or tempt me to do foolish or hurtful things? Am I listening to authority figures who can help me, or do I believe I can figure out what's best on my own?

Content. Is the content I'm discovering, paying attention to, and even just scrolling past appropriate? Am I willing to dig deep, when appropriate, or am I always satisfied with information? Does this approach fit with who I say I want to be?

Thinking with Five Ls[7]

What are my loves? What am I for? What am I passionate about? What do I prioritize? Does my use of technology support or undermine my answers? Does it help me find other things I may want to prioritize? If your teen, for example, had her own vision greatly improved by vision screening, she may develop a passion for making sure underresourced kids get vision screening. She might spend some online time researching eye doctors in the area with the goal of asking them about donating time at the apartment complex by school.

What are my longings? What do I say I want? What do I need? What do I hear myself talk about a lot? What do I think about in the middle of the night? Does my use of technology support or undermine my answers? Does it help me find other things I may want or need? For example, a teen may state a goal of staying close with his grandparents, but he may not be making time to talk on the phone with them because he's so much more comfortable with texting. His grandparents may learn how to send him text messages, but he might realize that he needs to make time to use the communication tool that's most comfortable for them.

What are my loyalties? What are my commitments? What are my unchangeables at this point in my life? Does my use of technology help me stay committed? Does it link me with other things I may want to commit to? Does it undermine my commitments? For example, a teen may be committed to improving as a singer, so he spends time watching videos online demonstrating proper warm-up and breathing techniques.

What are my labors? Do I work hard at the things I say matter? Do my loves, longings, and loyalties show up here? Does my use of technology support my labors? Does it direct me to other things I may want to work hard at? Or does my tech use undermine the things I say that I care most about? For example, a teen might say that gaming is relatively unimportant but then invest many, many hours trying to get a higher score on a game. That would be laboring over something that is not a chosen priority.

What are my liturgies? What healthy habits and rhythms am I establishing for my life? Does my use of technology support my habits? Does it help me discover other habits I may want to establish? Does it undermine my values? For example, a teen boy might decide that he needs to start each morning with more than just a quick Bible verse and wants to make that an essential habit, so he asks his youth pastor and dad to text him passages to reflect on. At the end of the day, he shares with either his youth pastor or his dad how these verses affected his behavior and feelings through his day. This is a great example of technology reinforcing the healthy habits this teen has chosen—and for building and maintaining relationship with authority figures, too.

Thinking about Social media[8]

Am I seeking approval? Am I lonely or disappointed in how my day has gone and that's why I need approval now? Am I confused about who I really am and expecting online friends to help me figure it out by what they do and don't like? Would it be wiser to talk with someone offline about my feelings? Paul wrote, "Love rejoices with the truth" (1 Corinthians 13:6).

Am I boasting? There's a difference between bragging and sharing good news so people can share in our joy. If I'm feeling like I *need* others to know about something I've done, why do I? Paul wrote, "Love does not boast" (1 Corinthians 13:4).

Am I discontent? Why do I think posting something will help my attitude? Or do I not want help? Do I want people to attend my pity party instead? Scrolling our social media feeds can feed dissatisfaction and our discontentment can grow. Instead, I can ask what do I have to be grateful for and who can I talk with who will support me? Jesus wants us to find rest in Him when we are "weary and burdened" (Matthew 11:28). Paul reminds us to "carry each other's burdens" (Galatians 6:2), and he also teaches that love "always hopes" (1 Corinthians 13:7).

Is this a moment to protect? Why do I want to share something publically that could remain private? What would the other people involved think if I posted about it? What are the advantages of this remaining more intimate and just between us? Paul instructs that love "always protects" (1 Corinthians 13:7).

Is it kind? Although our culture may suggest we can

comment on anything we want and share whatever we want, we know better. Just because the Internet may make us feel safe, we still are responsible for what we communicate and how. Paul's list about love includes that "love is kind" (1 Corinthians 13:4), and Jesus instructs that we'll be known by our love (John 13:35).

Thinking about Relationships

Is my Internet activity reinforcing healthy relational perspectives? Am I viewing examples of truth and grace? Am I positive and optimistic when relating? Do I prioritize personal happiness too much when interacting? Am I speaking the truth in love and keeping things private that should be private? Am I reporting to adults things I should?

Are my online communities personally uplifting? After being on them awhile, am I more optimistic or pessimistic? More at peace or more agitated? More energized or apathetic? More content or discontented?

Would I want teens around me to follow my example of online activity and tech use? Am I making wise choices about who to connect with and why? Am I ending online relationships well that are no longer healthy? Is my use of technology a stumbling block for anyone?

Thinking about Stewardship

Am I too dependent on technology? Is it controlling me, or am I controlling it? Do I use it appropriately and also use offline resources in tandem and appropriately? Am I wasting more time than is appropriate with my technology? Do I think technology can make me or keep me happy and that's why I use it when and how I do? Would it help if I learned how to handle quiet and solitude better?

Are all these screens necessary? In what ways do they increase my quality of life? Are they taking over my life in any way? What are some healthy and enjoyable nontech things I can intentionally make time for?

Am I on too many social networks? Should I just choose one and become a better steward of my time and then maybe add another? Are my reasons for wanting to be on another appropriate?

Is my use of technology, including the Internet, flooding my spirit with desensitizing messages and stimuli? Am I no longer bothered by conversations or visuals that used to upset me? Am I able to filter out harmful messages or content? Am I letting things slide and not blocking what I used to?

Thinking about Spiritual Growth

Do the consistent messages I receive through my social media feeds, emails, texts, and news alerts support my biblical values, love for God, and Christian worldview? Are these healthy, helpful, harmful?

Is my online activity or use of other technology causing my heart to wander in a spiritual sense? Do I feel closer, more distant, or unaffected in my relationship to God? Am I thinking with a Christian worldview more or less than before? Am I satisfied with the "Verse of the Day" or do I take time to study God's Word?

When online or engrossed in a game or other technology, do temptations (of any sort) increase? Do I need to change what I do? Talk to anyone? Can I steward my time and attention in other ways?

Am I using technology to impart grace, love, and life in Jesus' name? Is God pleased with how I'm stewarding my screen time and technology? Are there things I could do intentionally to spread the Gospel and help others mature in their faith specifically through technology?

I pray you're not overwhelmed by what seems like a long list of questions! These questions are meant only to spark and shape your thinking, together with your teen. They're certainly not meant to become the basis of interrogating your teens. Use them as parameters for your own tech life, perhaps openly sharing with your teens how you respond to the questions. Perhaps your teen will feel ready to incorporate some of these questions in his or her thinking about technology.

ALERT AND INVOLVED

Depending on your age, I imagine you've gone from one type of phone to another, from desktop computers to laptops and tablets, and from one gaming system to another. And there'll be something new before we know it! No matter what tools and toys come our way, as adults who care about young people, we have to commit to stay alert and involved.

Nehemiah and Mordecai are two Old Testament heroes of mine. They provide an excellent example of what happens when God's people stay alert and get involved.

Nehemiah saw Israel in exile trying to reconnect with their roots and trying to reunify their hearts by rebuilding their home. He didn't despair and do nothing. He wept (Nehemiah 1:4). He prayed regularly (1:6), beginning with praise about God (1:5). He admitted where he had sinned and fallen short (1:6). He planned (2:5ff). He motivated people to work with their whole hearts (4:6). The environment around him threw every distraction and obstacle possible at Israel. Yet Nehemiah courageously persevered, and the family of God was preserved and strengthened. The ways he dealt with these distractions and kept his focus inspires me.

And then there's Mordecai, Esther's older cousin, who raised her when she was orphaned. If you read the book of Esther, you'll see that he remained present in her life when she was recruited to possibly be the next queen (Esther 2:11, 21–23). He provided more than advice; he instructed her (2:10). Esther learned his wise counsel could be trusted (2:20). Mordecai challenged her to do great things (4:4–8, 12–14). Her following through on "such a time as this" ultimately saved the Jewish people (4:14–17). If you read this book through Mordecai's eyes rather than Esther's, you'll learn much about parenting well during difficult times. As I often say, today's Esthers need a Mordecai.

Today technology and the Internet are part of home life, with all the good and bad that brings. The voices, noises, screens, and distractions of our culture can sometimes feel like a tsunami threatening the security of our homes and children. However, we can defend our families against the lies. We can be proactive and engaged in leading our teens with intention. Equipped with truth, we will expose the lies and battle for the hearts and minds of teens. What could be a better use for our time, effort, and energy? We can and we will connect with our kids in this wireless world.

> Remember the Lord, who is great and awesome,
> and fight for your families.
>
> NEHEMIAH 4:14

DISCUSSION GUIDE

People of all ages—parents, grandparents, volunteers, teachers —come together because they care about this technology-saturated generation. Knowing we're not alone with our questions and concerns is a huge comfort. Beyond that, parents and their teens may use these discussion questions to help jumpstart some teachable moments about technology.

CHAPTER 1 • TECHNOLOGY
AND OUR DEEPEST HUMAN NEEDS

1. Over the years of your life, which new technology has sparked the most dramatic lifestyle change for you? What has been your favorite new technological tool?
2. How do you see the speed of technology changes affecting your family's life? Do you think your children are aware of these effects? How can you tell?

3. Every family experiences pressures. Are any of your family's current sources of pressure potentially linked to technology use? Are they pressuring parents, teens, or both? Do any immediate solutions spring to mind?

4. In what ways do you see digital tools enhancing your family life? How is it a particular blessing to you or to your teens?

5. Have you or your teens increased your dependence on technology so much that you turn to it to meet most of your needs? How is this dependence/trust/attention similar to worship? What is a more rightful place for technology, in your opinion?

6. Does being cut off from access to technology feel like a threat to your security?

7. How does your online/digital use define you as a person? Is your sense of self online different from your identity in the flesh-and-bone world? Do you think social media has affected your view of your identity?

8. Where would you say you feel most at home, comforted, and securely belonging? Do you feel more connected with your online interactions or out and about with people? Does home provide healthy belonging for you? What about your church family?

9. Where have you, as a parent, identified your purpose in life? Do you think your teens are aware of their purpose? What's the evidence? Whether they have or haven't yet discovered their purpose, how has technology been relevant?

10. Do the "perfect" posts you see on social media ever threaten your own belief in your competency? For you, does the best-foot-forward nature of social media posts feed perfectionism or make you feel like giving up?

CHAPTER 2 • TRUTHS ABOUT TODAY'S TEENS

1. Do you think you have belief-based relationships or relationship-based beliefs? What about your teens? If there's a difference in your approaches to your values, how do they play out in your decisions or in those of your teen?

2. When have you encountered teens who were passionate about changing the world? Has exposure through technology ever sparked your interest in a cause or led you to world-changing aspirations? Can you share some details?

3. Do you see the creative, innovative, entrepreneurial spirit in your teens or in their peers? How has this gift led to blessings for your family or others? Can you see any downside to this kind of innovative thinking? What would that be?

4. Do you ever feel stressed or overwhelmed after spending time with the tools of technology? Which tools? Are there other factors? Do you see signs in your teens that their tech use contributes to their stress? How might you be able to talk with them about the connections?

5. How can technology lead to fatigue? When have you noticed tech-related tiredness affecting your family members? What success have you had in dealing with the problem? Have you

already found ways to bring any of this up with your teens? How did that go?

6. More and more young people are experiencing depression or anxiety issues. If you have ever struggled with depression, to what coping behaviors did you default? Do you see your teens turning to digital tools to cope with stress or distress?

7. What differences do you see between the challenges kids face today and the ones you faced when you were a teen? What gives you hope about the future? Do you think your teens experience a similar hope? Why or why not?

CHAPTER 3 • LESS AND MORE

1. Sherry Turkle wrote, "Technology doesn't just do things for us. It does things to us, changing not just what we do but who we are." What changes have you seen in yourself that might be explained by technology? Have you seen similar changes in your teenagers?

2. What would be a good method for your family to use for determining how to incorporate face-to-face connecting zones and face-to-face connecting days? Could you set a time for doing this?

3. Have you ever given yourself a media-free time out? How did you feel during your time without screen access? Was the experiment valuable for you?

4. Do you catch yourself living through the lens—that is, taking so many photos with your phone or camera that you

actually missed aspects of what was going on around you? Does perfectionism play into your photo-taking or your photo-sharing?

5. Do you think you were self-centered during some part of your own teen years? What might be some contributing factors to the self-focus you see in your teens?

6. Where do you incorporate quiet during the average day, or during the average week? What do you think about when you're surrounded by quiet? How might you find more ways to fit times of silence into your family's week?

7. Does your family have good memories of times when you read together? What were the favorite stories? Do you still share in reading together or listening to audiobooks?

8. How can boredom be positive?

9. What ways has your family continued to find ways to play together?

10. When have you felt most thankful? Do you see your teenagers discovering the gratitude attitude, or is this an area of challenge for your family? What practices have you found that reinforce your feelings of thankfulness?

CHAPTER 4 • LIE #1: I AM THE
CENTER OF MY OWN UNIVERSE

1. If you had to come up with a different name for the center-of-the-universe lie, what would it be?

2. In general terms, do you think self-at-the-center is a common way to view the world? What evidence do you see in the culture at large that this worldview is in operation? Do you see it at home, too?

3. If you are familiar with the Bible, brainstorm some principles you know from God's Word that refute the lie that each person is the center of his or her own universe.

4. Was there a time when you overprioritized your children? Did you see any negative results for you? For them?

5. How do tech tools broaden awareness of the wider world and its needs? How could overuse of tech tools contribute to a self-at-the-center mentality?

6. What makes personal relationships offline more meaningful to you than your online friendships? Which interpersonal skills can develop only in person-to-person contact?

CHAPTER 5 • LIE #2: I DESERVE
TO BE HAPPY ALL THE TIME

1. While you probably would never say the actual words *I deserve to be happy all the time,* when do you see yourself falling into a pattern of thinking or acting this way?

2. Do you see any FOMO (fear of missing out) behaviors associated with technology use at your house?

3. When you have instituted screen-free times for your family, about how long does it take for everyone to calm down, shift their focus, and engage with the family? What good results

have you seen from screen-free times with your family?

4. As technology has reduced waiting time in so many aspects of everyday life, have you found yourself increasingly impatient? Give an example of when you notice this in yourself.

5. When have you found it hard to discipline yourself to tackling something difficult or tedious? Do your teens know you experience frustration and weariness when it comes to some of the tasks in your life? When have you seen your teens give up easily? When have they worked hard and found it gratifying?

6. What nontech activities do the teens and adults in your family enjoy? Brainstorm an additional list right now.

7. What actions lead to negative disciplinary consequences in your family? Dr. Kathy talks about establishing ground rules and then using language that reinforces the teen's responsibility of choosing: "You chose a good path. You did well." Or, "Your decision led to trouble." What good results could come from emphasizing the teen's ability to choose?

8. What have been some "growth points" in your teen's life—times when he or she struggled with an issue and really came through it with positive changes? Have you been able to talk with your teen to affirm his or her choices and actions during that time?

CHAPTER 6 • LIE #3: I MUST HAVE CHOICES

1. Would you say that variety has always been everyone's spice of life, or do you think today's multiple available choices feed

a bigger demand for options? When have you seen this in action?

2. Have you personally ever been overwhelmed when faced with too many options? When have you seen this happen to your teen?

3. When have you been able to sort or narrow a range of options for your teen who is faced with a big decision? What other ways have you been able to participate in your teen's decision-making?

4. If you are familiar with the Bible, can you think of specific principles or verses that promote contentment as opposed to demand for choices? Brainstorm some of these now.

5. Does your teen show an interest in meeting others' needs? How could you incorporate more opportunities to serve those who are needy, physically or emotionally?

6. On a scale of one to ten, what's the grumble factor in your household? How do you, as a parent, contribute to the complaining and arguing that take place? What works for you when you feel like complaining? How have you been able to help your kids refrain from arguing and complaining?

7. Remember the description that called multitasking a "continual, partial attention"? When do you fall into that pattern? Do you see it happening with your teen? When are you most able to concentrate and focus on only one need or idea?

8. Take a guess. How do you think your teen would answer the question, "What problems would you like to help solve?"

Brainstorm a time this week when you might actually ask your teen this question.

CHAPTER 7 • LIE #4: I AM MY OWN AUTHORITY

1. If you were going to rename this authority lie, what would you call it?

2. Despite your best efforts, when have you been a Friend Parent, an Absent Parent, or an Inconsistent Parent? When have you found the best balance of consistent and gentle authoritative parenting? What goes right when you're consistent in exercising loving authority?

3. You have probably noticed authority figures being ridiculed on television or at the movies. When have your kids noticed and mentioned this trend? Have you ever seen behaviors in your family that mimic that disrespect for parents and other authorities? How have you been able to help your kids show respect for parents and teachers?

4. If you are familiar with the Bible, brainstorm truths you know from God's Word that talk about how people should relate to authority. When have you seen some of these positive principles at work?

5. What kinds of authority figures are currently part of your teen's life? Do these people handle their position wisely and well? How do your teens relate to their use of power, whether it's good or bad?

6. When do you find it easiest to submit to authority—God's

authority, a boss's authority, a teacher's authority, the church leadership? What do leaders do to make it easier for you to submit to their authority over you?

CHAPTER 8 • LIE #5: INFORMATION IS ALL I NEED SO I DON'T NEED TEACHERS

1. How would you define *information*? Does that definition differ from the definition for *knowledge* or the definition of *wisdom*?

2. Who have been your most influential teachers over the course of your life? What made their teaching so meaningful for you?

3. When has your teen's intuitive understanding of tech tools been a blessing for your family? Were you able to articulate your thanks to your teen for sharing that expertise?

4. What is good about self-sufficiency? Are there areas in which we should encourage teens to be self-sufficient? How does self-sufficiency relate to living in community? In what ways should we encourage teens to develop dependence on others?

5. When have you, as an adult, had to accept critique and be teachable? What was painful about that experience? What blessings came from that time?

6. If you are familiar with the Bible, what concepts have you encountered in God's Word that seemed paradoxical? How have you been able to grow in your faith despite these complexities?

7. When have you been able to help your teens sort and sift a load of information that's before them? Did your teen welcome your assistance? When have you been able to help your teen make connections between apparently disconnected bits of information or seemingly unrelated ideas? Was your teen able to understand the synthesis of ideas when you explained your insight?

CHAPTER 9 • THE ULTIMATE CONNECTIVITY

1. Who are the people with whom you share your deepest connection? When have you felt strongly connected to your teen? Do you think your teen felt the connection at the same time?

2. Why is it worth putting in a lot of effort to build a deep, meaningful connection with your teen? What would you miss if this connection gets broken or damaged?

3. How have you been able to improve your connection with your teen using the tools of technology? How do you see the tech tools and other relationship skills working together?

4. Questions are a definite asset when it comes to sparking conversation between parents and teens. But have you ever felt overwhelmed by questions coming at you? Have you ever slid into interrogation mode when addressing your teen? Why are questions delivered in a barrage so much less effective than gentle questioning mixed with other comments and interaction?

5. When and where have your best conversations with your teen taken place? Have you ever tried to re-create some of those conditions in order to initiate another deep interaction with your son or daughter? How did that work?

6. How might conversations with Mom and Dad help to meet the five deep human needs of security, identity, belonging, purpose, and competence?

7. Now that you've reached the end of this book, have you identified ways your teens need more guidance in their technology use? What made you aware of this? What changes do you hope to implement at home?

8. Which categories of questions did you think would be most effective with your particular teen—maybe the Four Cs or the Five Ls? Which of these might be the best category to begin to discuss with your teen—social media, relationships, stewardship, or spiritual growth? How might you get your teens on board for a time of talking through some of the questions included in this chapter, a few at a time?

9. As you've explored some of these technology-related issues, your own worldview and its implications have come under the microscope, to some degree. Have you surprised yourself by discovering any discrepancies between your stated beliefs and your actual practices? Are you able to talk with your teens about your own pursuit of integrity between your behaviors and your heart?

10. If you could narrow it down to one growth point, what would be your most useful takeaway from spending time in the teaching of this book? Are you hopeful about the changes you plan for your family?

How can we help you? Visit us at www.ScreensAndTeens.com for more information, more tools, and a place to share ideas with other parents of teens.

NOTES

Chapter 1 • Technology and Our Deepest Human Needs

1. "Read Schuchardt on Media, Tech, and Religion," The Christian Leadership Center Blog, University of Mary (November 29, 2011). www.clcumary.com.

2. We find our security in God. See John 14:6, 1 John 5:18, and Romans 8:1–2.

3. "I urge you, brothers and sisters, in view of God's mercy, to offer your bodies as a living sacrifice, holy and pleasing to God—this is your true and proper worship" (Romans 12:1).

4. On belonging to God: John 1:12, Colossians 2:10, Colossians 3:3.

5. Our purpose is to glorify God: Isaiah 43:7, John 15:16.

6. Unique purpose: John 15:5, Ephesians 2:10.

7. I look forward to interacting with you on the website designed for this book, answering questions and hearing your stories. Look for information, updates, and resources at www.ScreensAndTeens.com.

Chapter 2 • Truths about Today's Teens

1. Alan Kay, Brainyquote.com.

2. "Making Connections—Wiring the Brain," Better Brains for Babies, University of Georgia (2014). http://spock.fcs.uga.edu.

3. Ibid.

4. Scott Degraffenreid, *Understanding the Millennial Mind: A Menace or Amazing?* (Dallas: N2Millennials, 2008), 14.

5. Transformed minds: Romans 12:2, Colossians 3:10, Ephesians 4:22–24.

6. Alisa Harris, "Technology: Online Tools Are Reshaping the Way Young Americans Go about Trying to Change the World," *World* 24, no. 2 (January 31, 2009).

7. "What Is Addiction? What Causes Addiction?" Medical News Today Blog (March 2009). www.medicalnewstoday.com.

8. Sarah Cassidy, "The Online Generation: Four in 10 Children Are Addicted to the Internet," *The Independent* (May 9, 2014). www.independent.co.uk.

9. Ibid.

10. Chris Rowan, "10 Reasons Why Handheld Devices Should Be Banned for Children under the Age of 12," *Huffington Post* (March 6, 2014). www.huffingtonpost.com.

11. National Center on Addiction and Substance Abuse, "Adolescent Substance Use: America's #1 Public Health Problem," New York: The National Center on Addiction and Substance Abuse at Columbia University, 39, table 99, June 2011, www.casacolumbia.org.

12. Ibid.

13. Sarah Cassidy, "The Online Generation."

14. Rebecca Hiscott, "8 Ways Tech Has Completely Rewired Our Brains," *Mashable,* March 14, 2014, www.mashable.com.

15. Chris Rowan, "10 Reasons."

16. Barry Schwartz, "The Paradox of Choice," Ted Talk (July 2005). www.ted.com.

17. "Stress Statistics," Statistic Brain, July 8, 2014, www.statisticbrain.com.

18. Josh James, "Data Never Sleeps 2.0," Domosphere, April 23, 2014, www.domo.com.

19. Laura Kann, Steve Kinchen, Shari Shanklin, et al., "Youth Risk Behavior Surveillance—United States, 2013," *Morbidity and Mortality Weekly Report* (MMWR) 2014; 63 (no. 4: 13, 72).

20. Centers for Disease Control and Prevention, "Suicide Prevention: Youth Suicide," January 9, 2014, www.cdc.gov.

21. Ibid.

22. Laura Kann, et al., "Youth Risk Behavior," 2.

Chapter 3 • Less and More

1. Sherry Turkle, "The Documented Life," *New York Times,* December 16, 2013, www.nytimes.com.

2. Jenae Jacobson, "The iPad Is Stealing My Son's Childhood," *I Can Teach My Child Blog,* June 8, 2014, www.ICanTeachMyChild.com.

3. Gary Chapman and Arlene Pellicane, *Growing Up Social: Raising Relational Kids in a Screen-Driven World* (Chicago: Moody Publishers, 2014), 171.

4. Randi Zuckerberg, "Randi Zuckerberg Discusses the Hazards of Social media," *New York Daily News,* November 5, 2013, www.nydailynews.com.

5. Catherine Steiner-Adair and Teresa Barker, *The Big Disconnect: Protecting Childhood And Family Relationships in the Digital Age* (New York: Harper, 2013), 4.

6. Renee Robinson, "A Letter to My Boys (The Real Reason I Say No to Electronics), blog repost, May 27, 2014, www.renee-robinson.com.

7. Archibald D. Hart and Sylvia Hart Frejd, *The Digital Invasion: How Technology Is Shaping You and Your Relationships* (Grand Rapids: Baker Books, 2013), 72.

8. Personal story from Jill Savage.

9. Jenae Jacobson, "The iPad is Stealing My Son's Childhood."

10. Mark Memmott, "Picture This: Selfie Is 'Word of the Year,'" National Public Radio, November 19, 2013, www.npr.org.

11. *CPYU Parent Page* (Elizabethtown, PA: Center for Parent/Youth Understanding), November 2013, 3.

12. Richard C. Anderson, Elfrieda H. Hiebert, Judith A. Scott, and Ian A. G. Wilkinson, *Becoming a Nation of Readers* (Washington, D.C.: National Institute of Education, 1985).

13. Archibald D. Hart and Sylvia Hart Frejd, *Digital Invasion,* 67.

14. Catherine Steiner-Adair and Teresa Barker, *Big Disconnect,* 275.

15. Lesley Brown (Ed), *The New Shorter Oxford English Dictionary on Historical Principles,* vol. 2 N–Z (New York: Oxford University Press, 1993).

Chapter 4 • Lie #1: I Am the Center of My Own Universe

1. Sue Bohlin, "What Is a Worldview?" Probe Ministries, 2011, www.probe.org.

2. Ibid.

3. Marshall McLuhan, "Biography," www.marshallmcluhan.com.

4. Jill Savage and Kathy Koch, *No More Perfect Kids: Love Your Kids for Who They Are* (Chicago: Moody Publishers, 2014), 107.

5. Ibid.

6. The world is about God and for Him: Isaiah 41:18–21, Colossians 1:16.

7. To explore types of intelligence, see my book *How Am I Smart? A Parent's Guide to Multiple Intelligences* (Chicago: Moody Publishers, 2007) or look for the pocket guide about the "smarts" at www.CelebrateKids.com.

8. Jill Savage and Kathy Koch, *No More Perfect Kids,* chap. 5.

9. Catherine Steiner-Adair and Teresa Barker, *The Big Disconnect* (New York: Harper, 2013), 201.

10. Gary Chapman and Arlene Pellicane, *Growing Up Social,* 36.

11. To read more on this subject, see chapter 6 of my book *Finding Authentic Hope and Wholeness* (Chicago: Moody Publishers, 2005) or look for more information at www.ScreensAndTeens.com.

12. For more help with friendship levels, go to ScreensAndTeens.com for sample questions to use when determining if someone should be moved to a new level of intimacy. CelebrateKids.com also offers a pamphlet *Relationships to Friendships.*

13. To learn more about body language cues, check out the chapter called "People Smart" in my book *How Am I Smart?* (Chicago: Moody Publishers, 2007).

14. There are 41 one-another commands in the New Testament about how to relate. You can find their references at www.ScreensAndTeens.com.

15. Patricia Hersch, *A Tribe Apart: A Journey into the Heart of American Adolescence* (New York: Fawcett Columbine, 1998), 222.

Chapter 5 • Lie #2: I Deserve to Be Happy All the Time

1. Scott Degraffenreid, *Understanding the Millennial Mind* (Dallas: N2Millenials, 2008), 28.

2. Ibid., 58.

3. Galatians 5:22–23.

4. Philippians 4:13 ESV.

5. University of Kentucky, "But They Did Not Give Up," www.uky.edu.

6. Psalm 5:3, Psalm 33:20, Psalm 37:7, Psalm 38:15, Psalm 40:1, Micah 7:7, Ephesians 3:20.

7. Jill Savage and Kathy Koch, *No More Perfect Kids: Love Your Kids for Who They Are* (Chicago: Moody Publishers, 2014), 186.

8. Gary Chapman and Arlene Pellicane, *Growing Up Social: Raising Relational Kids in a Screen-Driven World* (Chicago: Moody Publishers, 2014), 29.

9. See explanation of the core needs in chapter 1. My book *Finding Authentic Hope and Wholeness: Five Questions That Will Change Your Life* (Chicago: Moody Publishers, 2005) unpacks these five core needs in great detail.

10. The topics of correcting and complimenting are covered in chapters 6 and 9 in *No More Perfect Kids.* I offer a CD on this topic on my website and a booklet that explains how to compliment effectively and teaches the difference between

correcting and criticizing. This also includes more than 400 words to use to help you transition from "good" and "bad" to adjectives that are much more helpful.

11. God will equip us to fulfill our purpose and finish our work (Philippians 1:6). We're created in advance to do good works (Ephesians 2:10) and empowered by His wisdom (James 1:5), strength (Isaiah 40:29), and love (Joshua 23:11).

12. Jill Savage and Kathy Koch, *No More Perfect Kids*, 185–86.

13. "High School Dropout Statistics," Statistic Brain, January 1, 2014, www.statisticbrain.com.

14. Pat Higgins, "National College Dropout Rate Increases," *The Duquesne Duke*, January 30, 2013, www.theduquesneduke.com.

15. Marc Graser, "Animated Hit Breaks Digital Record," March 19, 2014, www.variety.com.

16. Daniel Nye Griffiths, "Activision Boasts $1 Billion 'Call of Duty: Ghosts' Day One Sales," *Forbes*, November 6, 2013, www.forbes.com.

17. Jill and Mark Savage, *Living with Less So Your Family Has More* (Guideposts Books, 2010).

18. Download a free Financial Notebook for Parents and Teens at www.jillsavage.org.

19. Gary Chapman and Arlene Pellicane, *Growing Up Social*, 55.

20. Erin Long, "6 Small Habits to Increase Contentment When Life Isn't Easy," *Red and Honey Blog*, July 11, 2014, www.redandhoney.com.

21. Anonymous, "Students and Video Game Addiction," *Inside Higher Education*, December 12, 2012, www.insidehighered.com. See also Nicholas Carr, *The Shallows: What the Internet Is Doing to Our Brains* (New York: Norton, 2010), 17–35.

22. Maria Popova, "Presence, Not Praise: How to Cultivate a Healthy Relationship with Achievement," *BrainPickings*, May 23, 2013, www.brainpickings.org.

23. Ibid.

24. Cara Joyner, "5 Questions to Ask Before Posting to Social Media," *Relevant*, January 14, 2014, www.relevantmagazine.com.

25. Sarah Brooks, "Parents: A Word About Instagram," *Life as of Late Blog*, April 28, 2013, www.lifeasoflate.com.

26. Ibid.

27. You can find a helpful list of emotions at the back of *No More Perfect Kids*. A teen can make a copy of this list and circle the words that best describe how they are feeling. This helps teens assess themselves and communicate with parents.

Chapter 6 • Lie #3: I Must Have Choices

1. Jill Savage and Kathy Koch, *No More Perfect Kids: Love Your Kids for Who They Are* (Chicago: Moody Publishers, 2014), 199.

2. Josh James, "Data Never Sleeps 2.0," Domosphere, April 23, 2014, www.domo.com.

3. "The New Golden Age of Radio," *AARP The Magazine* 57, no. 1A, December 2013/January 2014, 10.

4. "July 2014 Web Server Survey," July 31, 2014, www.news.netcraft.com.

5. Barry Schwartz, "The Paradox of Choice," Ted Talk, July 2005, www.ted.com.

6. Ibid.

7. Deuteronomy 6:6–8.

8. Kathy Koch, *Finding Authentic Hope and Wholeness: Five Questions That Will Change Your Life* (Chicago: Moody Publishers, 2005), chap. 4. See also Savage and Koch, *No More Perfect Kids* (Moody), chap. 6.

9. Joshua Becker, "Raising Consumer Conscious Teenagers in an Age of Excess," *Becoming Minimalist*. www.becomingminimalist.com.

10. Linda Stone, "Continuous Partial Attention," *Linda Stone*, 2014, http://lindastone.net.

11. Ibid.

12. Ron Alsop, *The Trophy Kids Grow Up: How the Millennial Generation Is Shaking Up the Workplace* (San Francisco: Jossey-Bass, 2008), 12, 115.

13. The gospel is simple: Jesus died for my sin and rose from the dead (Romans 5:8 and Ephesians 2:8–9). Click on "What Is the Gospel?" at www.evantell.org.

14. Eric Metaxas, "Taming Passions through Attention," *Breakpoint,* July 23, 2014, www.breakpoint.org.

15. 1 Corinthians 10:23, 2 Corinthians 3:17, Galatians 5:1.

Chapter 7 • Lie #4: I Am My Own Authority

1. See pluggedin.com for reviews of movies, videos, television shows, music, and games. You may also want to check out Bob Waliszewski's *Plugged-In Parenting: How to Raise Media-Savvy Kids with Love, Not War* (Carol Stream, IL: Tyndale House), 2011.

2. Here are links to blogs and websites that often report on issues relevant to young people disconnecting from the Christian community: www.barna.org, www.briandoddonleadership.com, www.canonandculture.com, www.charismanews.com, www.churchleaders.com, www.colsoncenter.org, www.cpyu.org,

www.fulleryouthinstitute.org, www.probe.org, www.stickyfaith.org,
www.summit.org, www.thomrainer.com.

Chapter 8 • Lie #5: Information Is All I Need So I Don't Need Teachers

1. Steven Spielberg, Quote of the Day, *Poddio*, July 23, 2014, http://podd.io.

2. Herman Horne, *Jesus the Teacher: Examining His Expertise in Education* (Grand Rapids: Kregel Publications, 1998).

3. See Proverbs 4:13, Proverbs 9:9, Matthew 11:29, 2 Timothy 3:16, Deuteronomy 4:9.

4. Many libraries offer short seminars on using databases and discerning levels of reliability on Internet research sources. This might be a worthwhile venture for a parent and teen to undertake together.

5. Janie B. Cheaney, "Generation Distraction," *World*, 29, no. 17, August 23, 2014.

6. *Webster's New World Dictionary and Thesaurus*, version 2.0 (New York: Macmillan Publishers; Colorado Springs, CO: Accent Software International, 1998).

7. Michael Youssef, "Wisdom from Heaven," *Leading the Way*, August 6, 2014, www.ltw.org.

8. Ibid.

9. See Matthew 19:16, John 14:16, and John 10:11. Jesus is called our Teacher, Counselor, and Good Shepherd for very good reasons.

10. David Kinnaman and Gabe Lyons, *UnChristian: What a New Generation Really Thinks about Christianity . . . and Why It Matters* (Grand Rapids: Baker Books, 2007), 125.

11. Jeff Myers, Paul Gutacker, and Paige Gutacker, *A Special Report: Unraveling the Mysteries of the Millennial Generation—How They Think, What They Believe, How They Relate, and How They Live* (Dayton, TN: Passing the Baton, Inc., 2010).

12. Archibald D. Hart and Sylvia Hart Frejd, *The Digital Invasion: How Technology Is Shaping You and Your Relationships* (Grand Rapids: Baker Books, 2013).

13. Gary Chapman and Arlene Pellicane, *Growing Up Social: Raising Relational Kids in a Screen-Driven World* (Chicago: Moody Publishers, 2014), 95.

14. Ibid, 97.

15. Sherry Turkle, "The Documented Life," *New York Times*, December 16, 2013, www.nytimes.com.

16. If you want specific suggestions, please check out our website at ScreensAndTeens.com.

17. Again, for more information about sifting, sorting, synthesizing, and sharing, go to ScreensAndTeens.com.

Chapter 9 • The Ultimate Connectivity

1. Catherine Steiner-Adair and Teresa Barker, *The Big Disconnect: Protecting Childhood And Family Relationships in the Digital Age* (New York: Harper, 2013), 13.

2. Sarah M. Coyne, Laura M. Padilla-Walker, Randal D. Day, James Harper, and Laura Stockdale, "Social Parenting: Teens Feel Closer to Parents When They Connect Online," *Cyberpsychology, Behavior, and Social Networking,* January 2014, 17(1): 8–13.

3. Brad Howell, "Using Social Media to Strengthen Family Bonds: A Practical Guide for Parents," Fuller Youth Institute, July 8, 2013, www.fulleryouthinstitute.org.

4. Gary Chapman and Arlene Pellicane, *Growing Up Social: Raising Relational Kids in a Screen-Driven World* (Chicago: Moody Publishers, 2014), 280.

5. Jill Savage and Kathy Koch, *No More Perfect Kids: Love Your Kids for Who They Are* (Chicago: Moody Publishers, 2014), 199.

6. Content included on typical contracts is posted at www.ScreensAndTeens.com if you want to use this to guide your conversations.

7. Adapted from John Stonestreet, "Cultivating Character: Connecting Right Belief to Right Behavior," Great Homeschool Convention, Ontario, CA, June 14, 2014.

8. Adapted from Cara Joyner, "5 Questions to Ask Before Posting to Social Media," *Relevant,* January 14, 2014, www.relevantmagazine.com.

ACKNOWLEDGMENTS

I have the best staff! Nancy, Linda, Randy, and Tina are passionate, skilled, and humble team members. Their support of me and the vision of Celebrate Kids, Inc., is humbling. They're among my favorite thought leaders, and I'm a better person for knowing them. I'm especially thankful for the care Nancy and Randy took to discuss the content of these pages with me and to edit my writing. This book is much better because of them. I'm grateful for others who reacted to some of my ideas, especially those who critiqued the chart in chapter 7.

I've learned much from Scott Degraffenreid and Brad Sargent regarding our younger generations, technology, and our culture. I'm grateful for their choice to invest in me.

Members of my board of directors are great examples of wisdom and sacrifice. They support and strengthen me with their prayers, questions, and ideas. I'm also grateful for family and friends who pray and believe for great things. Several friends reminded me regularly they were praying. Others reacted in helpful ways to respond to content I wanted their opinions about. Prayer warriors from my church and life group kept me going!

The staff and my other friends at Stonegate Fellowship in Midland, Texas, are a gift to me. I'm extremely grateful for their willingness and enthusiasm to host the recording of my *Screens and Teens* presentation. The panel members, video and audio tech staff, and all those who provide hospitality there so well are among my favorite people.

I'm honored to be represented by Ambassadors Speakers Bureau and am grateful for their work on my behalf. Speaking truths to thousands is still fun, invigorating, and a high privilege. I'm thankful for people who choose to hire me and for those in my audiences who keep me going and teach me so much as we interact.

I'm certainly grateful for my partnership with Jill Savage and Hearts at Home. Jill is supportive and wise. Hearts at Home conventions and publications are among the best things available for moms. I'm glad this book is a Hearts at Home imprint.

The team at Moody Publishers was easy to work with—and so supportive! This book is what it is because of their editorial expertise. I'm glad and grateful to be a Moody author.

Celebrate Kids is all about influence, so I'm glad to be connected with those who open doors so we can encourage and equip parents, grandparents, teachers, volunteers who work with kids, children of all ages, and others. My gratitude for God's love, power, and equipping is hard to put into words. (And, that's frustrating for a writer!) I'll just add that I love and trust Him. I'm so grateful for all He is and all He does!

Celebrate Kids, Inc. is dedicated to helping especially parents, educators, and children of all ages meet their core needs of security, identity, belonging, purpose, and competence in healthy ways. Through a problem-solving framework of these integrated needs, our programs and products provide solution-focused strategies that improve their intellectual, emotional, social, physical, and spiritual health.

Celebrate Kids helps parents, grandparents, teachers, administrators, pastors, and those who volunteer with children understand today's children and teens, value them, and help them use their strengths only for good and not to do harm.

Through presentations in churches, schools, conventions, and for organizations; online, live, and on-demand seminars; an extensive product line; our social media presence; and our bi-weekly email newsletter, we offer authentic hope for today and tomorrow and relevant solutions that work.

Dr. Kathy Koch founded Celebrate Kids in 1991, after serving as an elementary teacher, middle school coach, school board member, and university professor. Originally from Wauwatosa, a Milwaukee, WI, suburb, she moved to Fort Worth, TX, from Green Bay, WI, to fulfill God's purposes for her.

Email: Screens@CelebrateKids.com
Website: www.CelebrateKids.com
Blog: www.DrKathyKoch.com
Video: www.vimeo.com/channels/kathyisms
Facebook: www.facebook.com/celebratekidsinc
Pinterest: www.pinterest.com/kathycelebrate
Twitter: @DrKathyKoch
Website for this book: www.ScreensAndTeens.com

HEARTS at HOME

The Go-To Place for Moms

Hearts at Home's mission is to encourage, educate, and equip every mom in every season of motherhood using Christian values to strengthen families. Founded in 1993, Hearts at Home offers a variety of resources and events to assist women in their roles as wives and mothers.

Hearts at Home is designed to provide you with ongoing education and encouragement in your journey of motherhood. In addition to this book, our resources include the Heartbeat Radio Program and our extensive Hearts at Home website, blog, and eCommunity. We also offer a monthly free eNewsletter called *Hearts On-The-Go* as well as daily encouragement on Facebook and Twitter.

Additionally, Hearts at Home conference events make a great getaway for individuals, moms' groups, or for enjoying time with that special friend, sister, or sister-in-law. The regional conferences, attended by more than ten thousand women each year, provide a unique, affordable, and highly encouraging weekend for any mom in any season of motherhood.

Hearts at Home
1509 N. Clinton Blvd.
Bloomington, IL 61702
Phone: (309) 828–MOMS
E-mail: hearts@hearts-at-home.org
Web: www.hearts-at-home.org

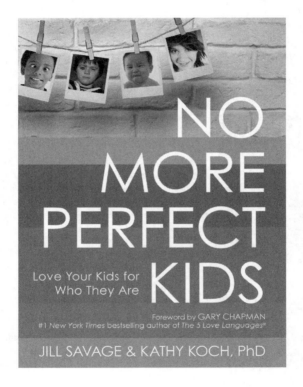

NO MORE PERFECT MOMS
Learn to Love Your Real Life

There is simply no such thing as a perfect mom. And there are no such things as perfect kids, perfect homes, perfect bodies, perfect marriages, or even perfect meals. With refreshing honesty, author Jill Savage exposes some of her own parental shortcomings with the goal of helping mothers everywhere shelve their desires for perfection along with their insecurities of not measuring up to other moms.

The 5 Love Languages of Children

Not only will Dr. Gary Chapman and Dr. Ross Campbell help you discover your child's love language, but you'll also learn how the love languages can help you discipline more effectively, build a foundation of unconditional love for your child, and understand the link between successful learning and the love languages.

The 5 Love Languages of Teenagers
The Secret to Loving Teens Effectively

It's easy to tell when a teenager wants to be loved. Getting the message across is another matter entirely. In addition to the obvious generation gap, many parents and children face a sort of language barrier as well. The 5 Love languages of Teenagers is an invaluable tool for analyzing a teen's love language and expressing your affections in an effective way. The search for love in a teenager's life can lead to disastrous results. But if you can speak the right language, the difference can seem miraculous.

AVAILABLE WHEREVER BOOKS ARE SOLD.

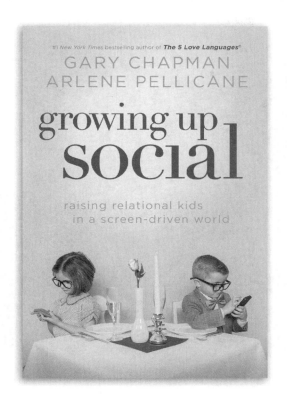

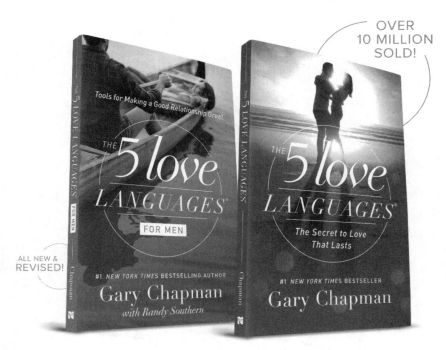